What the Qur'an Really Teaches About Jesus

Prophet of Allah or Savior of the World?

James K. Walker

HARVEST HOUSE PUBLISHERS
EUGENE, OREGON

Cover by Jason Gabbert Design

What the Qur'an Really Teaches About Jesus
Copyright © 2018 James K. Walker
Published by Harvest House Publishers
Eugene, Oregon 97408
www.harvesthousepublishers.com

ISBN 978-0-7369-7383-0 (pbk.)
ISBN 978-0-7369-7384-7 (eBook)

Library of Congress Cataloging-in-Publication Data

Names: Walker, James K., author.
Title: What the Qur'an really teaches about Jesus / James K. Walker.
Description: Eugene : Harvest House Publishers, 2018.
Identifiers: LCCN 2018009520 | ISBN 9780736973830 (pbk.)
Subjects: LCSH: Jesus Christ—Islamic interpretations. | Qur'an—Criticism, interpretation, etc. | Christianity and other religions--Islam. | Islam—Relations—Christianity.
Classification: LCC BP172 .W2534 2018 | DDC 297.2/465—dc23 LC record available at https://lccn.loc.gov/2018009520

Printed in the United States of America

18 19 20 21 22 23 24 25 26 / BP-SK / 10 9 8 7 6 5 4 3 2 1

Contents

Part 1:

Understanding Islam and the Qur'an

In Part 1, we will look at the significance of Islam as a major religion in world history and how it impacts almost every aspect of contemporary culture. We will lay out a brief history of Islam and the purported source, content, and basic teachings of its scripture, the Qur'an. We will see why it is essential for everyone, regardless of their religious background, to have at least a basic understanding of the beliefs of Islam and the teachings of the Qur'an.

Chapter 1

What Is Islam?

*Islam is a monotheistic religion, inviting all people to recognize,
believe, and worship God; believe in heaven and hell, believe in the
Day of Judgment; do what's right, forbid what's wrong; and follow
divine guidance. Islam is a universal message and religion. Islam is a
comprehensive way of life for anyone, anytime, and anywhere in the world.*

KHALIL MEEK, MUSLIM APOLOGIST
(Debate—see chapter 16)

Islam may be the fastest-growing religion in the history of the world. From an obscure, fledgling faith emerging from the Arabian Peninsula in the early seventh century, Islam quickly came to dominate the Middle East and north Africa before penetrating Europe, Asia, and the rest of the world. The recent growth of Islam in North America has been breathtaking. According to the latest US census, the Muslim population has jumped by 160 percent in just one decade.[1] Worldwide, Islam is already the second-largest world religion, and is now quickly closing in on two billion adherents.

Islam, however, is more than a religion. It is a culture, an ideology, a philosophy, an economic theory, a legal system, and much more. Islam is a way of life directly affecting one in four people in the world, and it is poised to become the major geopolitical issue of our generation. The religion plays a key role in contemporary events on the world stage, including global conflicts, unrest in the Mideast, religious terrorism, immigration controversies, and much more.

Unfortunately, the prominence of Islam and the controversy of radical Islamic terrorism have been marked by uneven coverage by the news media. Thus, in some cases, public perception about Muslims and their faith is being shaped by distortion or misinformation from the media, press, and even from prominent politicians and government leaders. The public in general—and Christians particularly—can be left with a faulty or incomplete understanding of Islam and its scripture, the Qur'an.

The impact of Islam on culture and world events should make understanding that faith a priority for all non-Muslims. For Christians, however, there is an additional motivation. By having a firm grasp on what the Qur'an actually says—and doesn't say—about Jesus, Christians can clearly see the essential differences between the two faiths. Knowing this, they will be equipped to begin gospel conversations about the Jesus of the Bible with their Muslim friends and neighbors.

A CRASH COURSE ON ISLAM

The religion of Islam is based primarily on their foundational scripture, the Qur'an,[2] which the prophet Muhammad claimed was dictated to him by the angel *Jibrīl* (Gabriel), initially in a cave on Mount Hira, near Mecca, in present-day Saudi Arabia. This scripture is divided into 114 *surahs* (chapters) containing more than 6,000 *ayats* (verses). Another important source of Islamic faith and practice is *Hadith,* collections of reported sayings and actions of Muhammad traced back to his trusted companions. There are two parts to each saying: *matn*—the saying itself, and *sanad*—the persons who form a chain from the compiler back to the person who purportedly heard Muhammad make the statement. Muslims have developed standards that enable them to evaluate both elements for probable accuracy.

The basic beliefs of Islam flow from essential monotheism and the doctrine that there is no God but God. Allah is the one true God of Islam, and there is no other. The word *Islam,* in Arabic, means "submission" or "submission to God (Allah)." One who submits to Allah is called a Muslim.

Tawhid is the foundation of Islamic monotheism and maintains that Allah is a unified "one," forever separate from creation. *Shirk* is the most serious sin in Islam, which involves ascribing any partnerships to God, such as "God the Father" or "God the Son,"[3] or ascribing the attributes of the one true creator God to anything or anyone else. Shirk is tantamount to idolatry in that it attributes that which is God's to that which is physical or created.

Sharia is the legal system of Islam and is the standard for both secular and religious law. A *fatwa* is an authoritative but nonbinding legal opinion given by a *mufti* (legal scholar).[4]

History

Muhammad was born about AD 570 into the Hashim clan of the Quraysh tribe in Mecca, on the Arabian Peninsula, in present-day Saudi Arabia. It is believed that his father, Abdullah, died before he was born, and his mother, Amina, died when Muhammad was only six. From that point onward he was raised by his uncle, Abu Talib. At age 25, Muhammad was hired by a wealthy widow, Khadijah, to lead a caravan to Syria. He later married Khadijah, and they had several sons, all of whom died in infancy, and four daughters.[5] Only one daughter, Fatimah, survived Muhammad.

While there were monotheists, including Christians and Jews, living in Arabia at the time, the majority of the people were polytheistic, and idolatry was rampant in Mecca. Muhammad claimed to have been sent by God to turn the people away from idolatry to worship the one true God and to take the correct path in life. There was much political opposition and persecution from the Meccan polytheists who largely rejected the prophet's message.

In AD 622, Muhammad and his small group of followers left Mecca and immigrated 210 miles north to Medina, in a journey called the *Hijrah*. In Medina, the prophet's message was more widely accepted, and Muhammad took on the role of political as well as spiritual leader. Jews who refused Muhammad's leadership were banished from Medina, or in some cases, sold as slaves or killed.[6] For years, warfare escalated between the Muslims of Medina and the Meccans, culminating in the final Muslim conquest of Mecca in AD 629 and its mass conversion to Islam.

In 632, a few years after conquering Mecca, Muhammad died. By that time, he had succeeded in uniting the majority of the Arabian Peninsula politically and spiritually under Islam. Immediately following the prophet's death, the new faith was led by a succession of four close companions and trusted advisors called the *Rashidun*, or the rightly guided caliphs. Disputes over leadership eventually led to *fitna* (upheaval or chaos), ultimately dividing Muslims into Sunni and Shia camps. Most accepted the leadership of all four caliphs and became known as Sunni, meaning "the path." A minority, however, rejected the authority of the first three caliphs, maintaining that the fourth caliph, Ali ibn Abi Talib (Muhammad's cousin and son-in-law), was actually the first Imam. This sect of Islam, the Shia,[7] believes that Ali and his descendants alone are the sole rightful successors to leadership of the Muslim people following the prophet's death.

Despite the schism, Islam continued to spread quickly through conquests of the lands that comprise present-day Afghanistan, Iraq, Iran, and north Africa. Eventually the message of Islam permeated much of Europe and Asia. Despite its rapid growth, Islam continued to be plagued by internal conflicts and infighting, sometimes marked by open violence and assassinations.

In a struggle to maintain a unified caliphate, the Umayyad dynasty was conquered by the Abbasid dynasty, which was eventually displaced by the great Ottoman Empire. In 1453, Muslim Turks conquered the city of Constantinople, and at its zenith in the seventeenth century, the Ottoman Empire controlled much of western Asia, north Africa, and southeastern Europe. Similar Islamic expansion occurred through the Mughal dynasty in India and south Asia as well as with the Shia in Persia (modern-day Iran) through the Safavid Empire in the sixteenth century.[8]

According to some estimates, by the twenty-first century, there were about 1.8 billion Muslims in the world.[9] Approximately 90 percent are Sunni, and 9 percent are Shia. The remaining 1 percent consists of various sects, including Sufism, a mystical/experiential form of Islam, and the Kharijites. As has happened with Christianity, splinter groups have broken away from Islam and claimed to be the true or ultimate expression of Islam—groups such as Ahmadiyya Islam[10] and the Nation of Islam.[11] In just 1,400 years of existence, Islam has grown to become the second-largest religion in the world.[12]

Doctrine

The word *Islam* means "submission," and one who submits to Allah is a Muslim. Muslims see Islam as the one true religion of God, which has always existed. Thus, the first prophet of Islam was not Muhammad, but the first man, Adam, who submitted to Allah and was therefore a Muslim. Muhammad is viewed as the final and greatest in a succession of prophets, including the biblical figures Adam, Moses, Abraham, David, and Jesus. Some Muslims claim that God sanctioned 124,000 prophets from Adam to Muhammad.[13]

Muslims maintain that they believe all the prophets, but that Muhammad is the final prophet, or the seal of the prophets, whom Allah used to restore the true teachings of the earlier prophets— teachings that allegedly had become altered or corrupted. Muslims believe in all the earlier revelations from God's prophets, particularly the Torah (the first five books of the Old Testament), the Psalms of David, and the Gospel (the teachings of Jesus).[14]

As will be further documented and discussed, Muslims believe in Jesus ('Îsa) as one of the prophets or messengers of Allah. They believe that He was born of a virgin and that He is the Messiah.[15]

However, they do not believe Jesus was God incarnate, or that He was the Son of God, as this would violate the tawhid of Allah and lead to the sin of shirk.[16] They also teach that Jesus was condemned to die on the cross but was never actually crucified, nor did He rise bodily from the dead.[17] The Qur'an places great emphasis on the final Day of Judgment and a literal heaven and hell. Salvation in Islam ultimately involves scales of justice on which one's sins are weighed against one's good deeds.[18]

Central to the proper practice of Islam are the five pillars of the faith, which are the duty of every faithful Muslim. There is an emphasis on performing each pillar properly with the correct form.

FIVE PILLARS OF ISLAM

Shahada (the Declaration)

The first pillar is a verbal confession of faith acknowledging Allah's uniqueness and Muhammad's status as prophet. The shahada, which is to be recited in Arabic, proclaims, "There is no God but Allah, and Muhammad is his prophet." Public confession of the shahada in Arabic is the first step to becoming a Muslim. To convert to Islam,[19] non-Arabic speakers are led by knowledgeable Muslims to properly repeat each Arabic word correctly.

Salat (the Prayers)

Muslims are to perform the obligatory prayers during five specific time periods each day. These five prayer times may sometimes be consolidated into three sessions. When possible, the prayers should be in the company of other Muslims in the *masjid* (mosque). Ritual washings precede each prayer, which is performed while facing Mecca. The head must be covered, and the prayers must be recited in Arabic. Great emphasis is placed on performing each step correctly with proper body posture while bowing.

Sawm (the Fast)

During Ramadan, the ninth month of the lunar calendar, Muslims are required to abstain from all food and liquids as well as sexual relations during daylight hours.[20] Muslims may awake early before sunrise for a meal before starting the fast, and each day's fast may end after sunset with a special meal called *iftar*. Ramadan ends with a three-day holiday called *Eid al-Fitr*.

Zakat (the Alms)

Each year, Muslims are required to contribute 2.5 percent of their wealth to the poor and oppressed (Surah 9:60). Muslim communities generally apply standardized rules for determining one's financial worth, and in Islamic countries, the government may collect the alms through a zakat tax.

Hajj (the Pilgrimage)

Unless prevented by poverty, it is the duty of every Muslim to make at least one spiritual journey to Mecca, Saudi Arabia, during *Dhu al-Hijjah*, the final month of the Islamic lunar calendar. During the hajj, Muslims perform rituals commemorating events in the life of Muhammad, Abraham, and others, including a ritual of stoning the devil, drinking from the Well of Zamzam, and performing the *tawaf*, marching counterclockwise seven times (circumambulating) around a black, cube-shaped structure known as the Kaaba. On each lap, participants point toward—or if possible, kiss—a black stone located on the eastern side of the Kaaba. It is believed that this stone dates back to Adam and Eve.

Jihad (the Struggle)

While not a pillar of Islam per se, jihad is an important principle for Muslims. Many Americans were introduced to the term following the terrorist attacks of 9/11 as the Muslim hijackers were said to be waging a holy war, or jihad. The Arabic word is better defined as "strive," and is often used to describe the internal struggle or effort one exerts in submitting to Allah.[21] It is with this understanding that many Muslims minimize the "lesser jihad" of war against the infidels and emphasize the "greater jihad" of personal compliance and obedience to Allah. Nevertheless, the principle of jihad, in connection with warfare, is found in the Qur'an.[22]

In the famous "sword" passage Surah 9:5, the Qur'an also commands Muslims to fight, kill, or subdue idolaters and nonbelievers, saying, "Slay the Pagans wherever ye find them." Jews and Christians, called the "people of the book," are "cursed" and specifically targeted for warfare and subjugation (9:29-30). The Qur'an also promises paradise to faithful Muslims killed in battle for the cause of jihad (47:4-6; 48:16-17).

JESUS CHRIST: PROPHET OF ALLAH OR SAVIOR OF THE WORLD?

Like Christianity, Islam is a monotheistic religion promoting the worship of one true God. Islam also highly honors Jesus ('Îsa) as one of God's holy messengers. Nevertheless, Allah of Islam is not the same God who is worshipped by Christians. As will be thoroughly explained in later chapters, no Muslim would ever confess that Allah is the Father of our Lord Jesus Christ (Matthew 16:13-17), nor would they tolerate the Christian doctrine of the Trinity.

Likewise, the Jesus ('Îsa) of Islam is not the Christ of Christianity (2 Corinthians 11:4). Islam denies Christ's deity, incarnation, crucifixion, and resurrection—essential elements of His identity according to the Bible (John 1:1-14; Philippians 2:6-11; 1 Corinthians 15:3-8). Of most significance is the fact that the Jesus of the Qur'an is not the Savior of the world. Islam teaches that Jesus is not anyone's Savior—Muslim or Christian. In fact, it could be argued that there is no Savior in Islam.[23]

TO THE MUSLIM READER

To the Muslims who are reading this book, I want to express my appreciation for your willingness to consider these issues. I would urge you to also read and believe the Gospels (*Injil*) as preserved in the New Testament. In the Qur'an, all true followers of God are admonished to follow and obey the commands of Jesus (Surah 3:50-52). To follow Jesus's commands, one must know what they are. The commands of Jesus, however, are not recorded in the Qur'an. The New Testament does preserve the teachings and commands of Jesus in the four Gospels. They contain firsthand accounts written within the time frame of the historical events they record.[24]

The Qur'an itself affirms that the Bible is God's Word and suggests that the message of the Qur'an should be validated by comparing it with the Gospel teachings of Jesus previously "revealed" to the Christians who are called "the people of the gospel" (Surah 5:46-49; see also 6:91 and 21:105). This message of Jesus, according to the Bible, is that He is the Son of God (Matthew 16:13-17). He claimed to be one with the Father and to be God (John 10:30-33). If Jesus was a prophet of God, one should believe in His prophecies, including the prophecy of His own death and resurrection for the sins of the world (Mark 8:31).

TO THE CHRISTIAN READER

To the Christians who are reading this book, I want to thank you for caring about the Muslim people. I wish to encourage you to develop new friendships and strengthen any existing relationships you have with Muslim friends, family members, coworkers, and neighbors.

The following chapters provide a foundation to help Christians and Muslims understand what beliefs they share in common and, more importantly, where their beliefs differ. Christians will have more productive conversations when they accurately grasp the beliefs of their Muslim neighbors and have a better understanding of the teachings of the Qur'an. It is hoped that this book will further that understanding and serve as a catalyst for meaningful gospel conversations.

Finally, this book is not about proving points or winning arguments. Instead of merely refuting Muslims, Christians are encouraged to develop genuine relationships and be alert to every opportunity to demonstrate the gospel of their Lord Jesus Christ—both in word and deed.[25]

Chapter 2

What Is the Qur'an?

The Qur'an is totally the opposite of Christianity.

ZIA HASSAN, FORMER MUSLIM
(Interview—see chapter 17)

The holy book of the Islamic faith is the Qur'an. The word
Qur'an (also spelled Koran), in Arabic, means "the recitation."
Only the Qur'an in Arabic is considered authoritative. Translations
of the Qur'an are not considered to be on the same level as the
Qur'an in Arabic. In fact, a translation of the Qur'an is considered
merely an interpretation. For Muslims, the Qur'an is the very word
of Allah and a directive for living to all who submit to Allah.

> The month of Ramadan in which was revealed the
> Qur'an, a guidance for mankind and clear proofs for the
> guidance and the criterion (between right and wrong)...
> (Surah 2:185).

> Verily, this Qur'an guides to that which is most just and
> right and gives glad tidings to the believers (in the One-
> ness of Allah and His Messenger, Muhammad صلى الله
> عليه وسلم), who work deeds of righteousness, that they
> shall have a great reward (Paradise) (Surah 17:9).

In about AD 610, at the age of 40, Muhammad received his
first revelation while "on the way to Mina, two miles from the Holy

City of Makkah, on Jabl al-Nur…[at] the Cave Hira."[1] It was in this small cave that Muhammad meditated and reported that he heard the voice of the angel *Jibrīl* (Gabriel) commanding him to "recite." The angel dictated to Muhammad the first passage:

> Read! In the Name of your Lord Who has created (all that exists). He has created man from a clot (a piece of thick coagulated blood). Read! And your Lord is the Most Generous.
>
> Who has taught (the writing) by the pen.
>
> He has taught man that which he knew not (Surah 96:1-5).

Muhammad received the first verses on the seventeenth of Ramadan, which is the ninth month on the lunar calendar.[2] He continued to receive additional revelations for the next 23 years, and these were preserved mostly through oral tradition. The first chapters were given in Mecca and the later ones in Medina.

The Qur'an has a total of 114 chapters, called *surahs*, containing 6,236 verses, called *ayats*.[3] Surahs are arranged, generally, in order from the longest to the shortest. Every surah, except the ninth, begins with the Arabic word *Basmala*, which is translated, "In the name of God, Most Gracious, Most Merciful."

While reading the Qur'an, you may notice some versions of familiar Bible stories, but with some changes. However, you will not find a creation account, the story of Muhammad, or the history of the Muslim faith. What you will find is an emphasis on hell, which is mentioned 783 times, or every 7.8 verses. In comparison, the New Testament mentions hell only 74 times.[4] Allah's authorization of the Qur'an is mentioned about 100 times, and jihad or "sword verses" are mentioned about 150 times.[5]

During the life of Muhammad, the Qur'an was memorized and recited by the adherents of Islam. Some verses may have been recorded on pieces of bone, palm leaves, etc., but the Qur'an did not exist in book form. The event that forever changed the transmission of the Qur'an took place in the region known as Al-Yamama (in present-day Saudi Arabia). At the Battle of Yamama, in December 632, 700[6] Hafiz,[7] the best reciters, were killed. The deaths of the Hafiz caused Umar, a future caliph, to insist that Abu Bakr, the first rightly guided caliph,[8] commission a written manuscript of the Qur'an. Under the direction of Abu Bakr, Zaid ibn Thabit codified the Qur'an. However, this was not the only version of the Qur'an to appear in writing. Debate arose as other codices (or copies) began to surface.

The existence of multiple and conflicting copies of the Qur'an motivated Uthman (the third rightly guided caliph) to issue what is known as the Uthmanic Recension. Uthman formed a committee to compile the various versions of the Qur'an.[9] After editing the versions and forming a standardized Qur'an, he commanded that all other versions of the Qur'an be burned or boiled.[10] Uthman wanted to have one standard Qur'an, and he hoped to attain it through his recension. Accomplishing such a standardization would be difficult given the extant copies and fragments, which is why Uthman ordered the variant copies of the Qur'an to be destroyed.

The problem with Uthman's attempt to eradicate variant readings of the Qur'an is that it casts a shadow of doubt on the likelihood that the Qur'an we have today is what was allegedly delivered to Muhammad. The result is a long list of Muslims who claim variant readings of the Qur'an.[11] This causes significant problems for the Qur'an's attestation that it is the uncorrupted and unchanging word of God.[12]

Abrogation is another important feature of the Qur'an. *Nasikh* and *mansukh* are the two Arabic words promoting the different aspects of abrogation. *Nasikh* refers to the new, dominant passage that abrogates or supersedes the earlier verses. *Mansukh* refers to the older, obsolete passages that are now abrogated. The source you consult will determine which verses are seen as abrogated. One example, given by some Muslim scholars, includes what is said about marriage and adultery:

> The adulterer-fornicator marries not but an adulteress-fornicatress or a Mushrikah, and the adulteress-fornicatress none marries her except an adulterer-fornicator or a Muskrik [and that means that the man who agrees to marry (have a sexual relation with) a Mushrikah (female polytheist, pagan or idolatress) or a prostitute, then surely he is either an adulterer-fornicator, or a Mushrik (polytheist, pagan or idolater)...] Such a thing is forbidden to the believers (of Islamic Monotheism) (Surah 24:3) [Abrogated—Mansukh].

> And marry those among you who are single (i.e. a man who has no wife and the woman who has no husband) and (also marry) the Salihun (pious, fit and capable ones) of your (male) slaves and maid-servants (female slaves). If they be poor, Allah will enrich them out of His Bounty. And Allah is All-Sufficient for His creatures' needs, All-Knowing (about the state of the people) (Surah 24:32) [Abrogator—Nasikh].

While various Muslim scholars will debate whether this example is abrogation or not, the status of abrogation on other verses poses serious ramifications.

Arguably, the sword verses are the most contested among Muslims. Most Muslims agree that the teachings in the sword verses relate only to a specific group for a specific time. For example, early teachings from the Qur'an state that one should not be forced into a religion:

> There is no compulsion in religion. Verily, the Right Path has become distinct from the wrong path. Whoever disbelieves in Taghut and believes in Allah, then he has grasped the most trustworthy handhold that will

never break. And Allah is All-Hearer, All-Knower (Surah 2:256).

The Qur'an is clear that one should not be forced to become a Muslim, but later verses in the Qur'an seem to contradict this. There is a contingency of Muslims who view the earlier, more peaceful verses (like the one above), to have been abrogated by the later sword verses. These sword verses present a violent contrast to the earlier teachings in the Qur'an:

> Then when the Sacred Months (the 1st, 7th, 11th, and 12th months of the Islamic calendar) have passed, then kill the Mushrikun (See V.2:105) wherever you find them, and capture them and besiege them, and lie in wait for them in each and every ambush. But if they repent and perform As-Salat (Iqamat-as-Salat), and give Zakat, then leave their way free. Verily, Allah is Oft-Forgiving, Most Merciful (Surah 9:5).

> Fight against those who (1) believe not in Allah, (2) nor in the Last Day, (3) nor forbid that which has been forbidden by Allah and His Messenger Muhammad (صلى الله عليه وسلم) (4) and those who acknowledge not the religion of truth (i.e. Islam) among the people of the Scripture (Jews and Christians), until they pay the Jizyah with willing submission, and feel themselves subdued (Surah 9:29).

Views concerning abrogation vary among Muslim scholars. Some hold to the concept that the Qur'an may abrogate itself. Others believe that the Qur'an could abrogate the Sunnah (a record of the deeds of Muhammad) and vice versa. Some Muslim scholars believe that the Qur'an abrogates all previous Scriptures, specifically the Pentateuch and Gospels. There is even a contingency of Muslim scholars who do not believe in the concept of abrogation.[13]

Muslim scholars will often argue that the Bible also has instances of abrogation. For example, the dietary laws found in Leviticus 11:44-47 were abrogated by the vision Peter received in Acts 10:9-29,34-35. However, this should not be viewed as abrogation, but rather, as the consummation of God's plan for mankind and a fulfillment of prophecy. Other examples of consummation would include circumcision and Sabbath observance. The greatest example of this would be the promise God made of a Servant-Messiah who would bring a new covenant (Isaiah 53; Jeremiah 31:31-34; Hebrews 8:7-13).[14]

———— QUESTIONS FOR DISCUSSION ————

At the end of each chapter in this book, I will include discussion questions that can be asked in conversations you have with your Muslim coworkers, friends, or neighbors. These questions are designed to encourage thoughtful discussion and provide opportunities for you to engage in constructive dialogue that encourages clear thinking and may open the door for sharing more about Jesus, the Bible, and the Christian faith.

The Qur'an claims to be the unchanged word of Allah. Muslims hold the Qur'an as the source of guidance and criterion between what is right or wrong. Despite the Uthmanic Recension, Muslims accept the Qur'an, in Arabic, as the word delivered from Allah to Muhammad through *Jibrīl*. The Bible, in contrast to the Qur'an, is supported by thousands of extant manuscripts that provide a record of how God's Word has remained unchanged—a Word that is not abrogated but consummated from Genesis to Revelation.

- Why was it necessary for Uthman to burn old fragments of the Qur'an?

- How can you determine what verses of the Qur'an should be abrogated?

- In the Bible, God has given us the fulfillment of what was prophesied in Isaiah 53. Would you like to see the consummation of that prophecy as stated in 1 Peter 2:24-25?

> …He Himself [Jesus] bore our sins in His body on the cross, so that we might die to sin and live to righteousness; for by His wounds you were healed.[25] For you were continually straying like sheep, but now you have returned to the Shepherd and Guardian of your souls (1 Peter 2:24-25).

Part 2:

The Jesus of the Qur'an

In Part 2, we will learn what the Qur'an says and does not say about Jesus. We will compare biblical scriptures with the Qur'an to explore both the surprising similarities and the serious differences between the Jesus of Islam and the Jesus of Christianity. We will discover how both religions answer Christ's own crucial question, "Who do you say that I am?" (Matthew 16:15).

Chapter 3

Jesus of the Qur'an
Is a Prophet of God

Muslims love, respect, honor, and revere Jesus. Jesus is considered a great
messenger prophet. Jesus was born from the virgin Mary. Jesus is a word
from God; however, Muslims do not consider Jesus to be divine, and
Muslims do not consider Jesus to be the Son, in any literal sense, of God.

KHALIL MEEK, MUSLIM APOLOGIST
(Debate—see chapter 16)

The Qur'an mentions Jesus by name 25 times, and He is alluded to in many other places. It is clear even from a casual reading of the Qur'an that Jesus is highly revered as an important prophet or messenger (Arabic, *nabi* or *rasul*) sent by God.

> We gave Moses the Book and followed him up with a succession of messengers; We gave Jesus the son of Mary Clear (Signs) and strengthened him with the holy spirit. Is it that whenever there comes to you a messenger with what ye yourselves desire not, ye are puffed up with pride?—Some ye called impostors, and others ye slay! (Surah 2:87).

Jesus is presented in the Qur'an as one of a great succession of prophets and "warners" (Arabic, *natheer*) sent by Allah to forewarn all people throughout history about God's coming judgment and to point them to the right path, Islam. These messengers of Allah included the first man, Adam, and many others, like the prophet Hud (Surah 7:65), who is not mentioned in the Bible. Most of the prophets identified in the Qur'an, however, are men named in the Bible:

> Say (O Muslims): We believe in Allah and that which is revealed unto us and that which was revealed unto Abraham, and Ishmael, and Isaac, and Jacob, and the tribes, and that which Moses and Jesus received, and that which the prophets received from their Lord. We make no distinction between any of them, and unto Him we have surrendered (Surah 2:136).

Islam teaches that the ministry of Jesus was prophesied by the earlier prophets, and that He was in every way a true prophet who must be obeyed. In fact, those who truly submit to Allah are to make no preferential distinctions between any of Allah's prophets. This command to accept all the prophets without distinction is to be recited by Muslims (Surah 2:136). In Surah 3, Muhammad was also commanded to recite the command:

> Say (O Muhammad): We believe in Allah and that which is revealed unto us and that which was revealed unto Abraham and Ishmael and Isaac and Jacob and the tribes, and that which was vouchsafed unto Moses and Jesus and the prophets from their Lord. We make no distinction between any of them, and unto Him we have surrendered (Surah 3:84).

Thus, Muslims are not merely following the prophet Muhammad. Instead, Muslims are commanded in the Qur'an to obey all the prophets whom Allah sent throughout history.

> Then, We sent after them, Our Messengers, and We sent 'Iesa (Jesus)—son of Maryam (Mary), and gave him the

Injeel (Gospel). And We ordained in the hearts of those who followed him, compassion and mercy. But the Monasticism which they invented for themselves, We did not prescribe for them, but (they sought it) only to please Allah therewith, but that they did not observe it with the right observance. So We gave those among them who believed, their (due) reward, but many of them are Fasiqun (rebellious, disobedient to Allah).

O you who believe [in Musa (Moses) (i.e. Jews) and 'Iesa (Jesus) (i.e. Christians)]! Fear Allah, and believe too in His Messenger (Muhammad), He will give you a double portion of His Mercy, and He will give you a light by which you shall walk (straight), and He will forgive you. And Allah is Oft-Forgiving, Most Merciful (Surah 57:27-28).

Christians agree that Jesus was a prophet of God, but add that He was more than a prophet. Christians furthermore assert that we have the prophecies of Jesus today, and that many of His prophecies have already been fulfilled and others are yet to be fulfilled. Christians affirm that the prophecies of Jesus were recorded by the Gospel writers—Matthew, Mark, Luke, and John, and that the four Gospels we have today have accurately preserved those prophecies.

Thus Christians not only honor Jesus as a prophet of God, they also possess Scriptures containing copies of His prophecies. We have His prophecies as well as His sermons, teachings, parables, and warnings. This gives Christians the opportunity to evaluate, test, and affirm the teachings of Jesus. We can learn essential truths from both the prophecies that have already been fulfilled and those that are yet to be fulfilled.

According to Islam, when God revealed the Qur'an to Muhammad, He was affirming all the Scriptures before it, including the Old Testament, Torah, and the Gospel of Jesus.

It is He Who has sent down the Book (the Qur'an) to you (O Muhammad صلى الله عليه وسلم) with truth, confirming what came before it. And He sent down the Taurat (Torah) and the Injeel (Gospel) (Surah 3:3).

The Qur'an even quotes Jesus affirming that through His prophetic ministry, God was giving Him Scripture.

> He ['Îsa (Jesus)] said: "Verily I am a slave of Allah, He has given me the Scripture and made me a Prophet" (Surah 19:30).

The Qur'an also confirms that the teachings of Jesus were to be found in the written Gospel of Jesus, which is called the *Injil* in Arabic. In fact, they maintain that the Gospel of Jesus *(Injil* of *'Îsa)* was one of the Scriptures revealed by Allah before the Qur'an. The "people of the Gospel" (Christians) would be judged by what God had already revealed in that earlier Scripture.

Furthermore, Muslims are even instructed to "judge by them" (the "old Scriptures") what "Allah had revealed" rather than follow after their own vain desires.

> And in their footsteps, We sent 'Îsa (Jesus), son of Maryam (Mary), confirming the Taurat (Torah) that had come before him, and We gave him the Injeel (Gospel), in which was guidance and light and confirmation of the Taurat (Torah) that had come before it, a guidance and an admonition for Al-Muttaqun (the pious—See V.2:2).

> Let the people of the Injeel (Gospel) judge by what Allah has revealed therein. And whosoever does not judge by what Allah has revealed (then) such (people) are the Fasiqun [the rebellious i.e. disobedient (of a lesser degree)] to Allah.

> And We have sent down to you (O Muhammad صلى الله عليه وسلم) the Book (this Qur'an) in truth, confirming

the Scripture that came before it and Muhaymin (trust-worthy in highness and a witness) over it (old Scriptures). So judge among them by what Allah has revealed, and follow not their vain desires, diverging away from the truth that has come to you…(Surah 5:46-48).

In future chapters, we will examine some of the New Testament prophecies of Jesus, as well as some of the Old Testament prophecies predicting His coming. These prophecies will be invaluable for helping to assess the claim that Jesus was a prophet of God, and they will address other more fundamental questions about the identity of Jesus. These prophecies will inform us about the historical claims that Jesus was crucified and rose from the dead—both of which are rejected by the Qur'an. Most importantly, these prophecies will be the key to addressing the primary question of this book: Was Jesus merely a prophet, or was He the Savior of the world?

DID THE PEOPLE OF THE BOOK CORRUPT THE BIBLE?

As we have already seen, based on Surah 5:46-48 and similar Quranic passages, Muslims readily agree that Allah revealed the older biblical Scriptures (Torah and the Gospel) through the prophets that preceded Muhammad. Muslims, however, generally distrust or reject these prophecies, as they are recorded in the Old and New Testaments. The Bible, they argue, is no longer trustworthy because it was deliberately altered and corrupted by the "People of the Scriptures (Jews and Christians)" (Surah 3:75).

And verily, among them is a party who distort the Book with their tongues (as they read), so that you may think it is from the Book, but it is not from the Book, and they say: "This is from Allah," but it is not from Allah; and they speak a lie against Allah while they know it (Surah 3:78).

This charge of biblical corruption raises a number of important questions when discussing Jesus with Muslims. How can we affirm the prophecies of Jesus if they no longer exist? Of what value are the prophecies of Jesus for us today if we do not have access to them? Indeed, why would God allow the prophecies of Jesus to be destroyed or fatally altered?

Another important related issue is the dating of this alleged corruption of the Bible. Did this corruption happen before Muhammad, after Muhammad, or both?

WAS THE ALLEGED CORRUPTION BEFORE OR AFTER MUHAMMAD?

Before Muhammad?

It seems that this purported corruption of the Bible could not have happened before Muhammad. As we already discussed, Surah 5:46-48 commands the people to "judge by them" (the "old Scriptures") what "Allah had revealed." Thus, to evaluate the new prophecies of Muhammad, people had to verify what was written by the earlier prophets in the Torah and Gospel. We should be able to safely assume that God would not command us to judge Muhammad's prophecies by consulting Scriptures that had been corrupted and were untrustworthy.

After Muhammad?

If one interprets this assumed corruption of the Bible (Torah and Gospel) as a prophecy of the Qur'an that occurred sometime after Muhammad's lifetime, it is even more problematic. Muhammad revealed the Qur'an in the early seventh century (about AD

609–632). We now have copies of the New Testament, including all four Gospels, that are centuries older than when Muhammad was alive. For example, both *Codex Sinaiticus* and *Codex Vaticanus* are dated to the fourth century AD and contain the same prophecies and essentially the same text found in our modern Bible translations. Thus, any alleged corruption could not have taken place after Muhammad in the seventh century, or even after the fourth century, for that matter.

Going back much earlier, we also now have the Great Isaiah Scroll, the most important text of the Dead Sea scrolls collection. That scroll, made up of 17 parchments, contains the entire text of the book of Isaiah and has been reliably dated (by radiocarbon and paleography) to 100 BC or earlier. This scroll also affirms the reliability and accuracy of the book of Isaiah as found in our modern Bible translations.

Included in that scroll are numerous prophecies[1] about the Messiah that evidently contradict what the Qur'an says about Him. He would be "pierced for our transgressions," and "by his wounds, we are healed." Isaiah prophesied that God "has laid on him the iniquity of us all" (Isaiah 53:5-6 NIV).

We have ample evidence that our modern Bible translations contain essentially the same text and prophecies as those found in Muhammad's day and centuries earlier. When the Qur'an commands people to "judge" and verify the prophecies of Muhammad by the Scripture that came before him (Surah 5:46-48), we have access to those documents and can do exactly that. We find no evidence that the biblical Scriptures have been corrupted, and we have strong evidence that the texts we have today are reliable. Some of this evidence predates Muhammad and the Qur'an by centuries.

QUESTIONS FOR DISCUSSION

Christians agree with Muslims that Jesus was a prophet, but there are important distinctions between the two. While the Qur'an strongly asserts that Jesus was a prophet of God, it is significant that virtually none of the prophecies proclaimed by Jesus can be found in the Qur'an. This raises some important questions for Muslims:

- If Jesus was a prophet of Allah, what did He prophesy?
- Were the prophecies given by Jesus fulfilled by God?
- Where did God's people record the prophecies proclaimed by Jesus?
- If the "people of the book" corrupted the earlier Scriptures, when did that corruption happen—before or after Muhammad?

Chapter 4

Jesus of the Qur'an
Was Born of a Virgin

*His birth was unique, He was born of the virgin Mary and Spirit
of God, He was the Word of God, and He was performing miracles
that no other human could do—only God could do them.*

ZIA HASSAN, FORMER MUSLIM
(Interview—see chapter 17)

One of the surprising facts about the Qur'an is its emphasis on
the virgin birth of Jesus. Mary, the mother of Jesus, is called
Maryam in the Qur'an. She is the only woman mentioned by name
in the Qur'an, and she is referenced 34 times—more times than in
the New Testament.

The emphasis in the four biblical Gospels is on the three-year
ministry of Jesus and especially the passion week leading up to His
crucifixion and resurrection. In the Qur'an, however, the major
focus is on the birth narrative and the infant baby Jesus, with very
little reported about His subsequent ministry or teachings.

There is a whole chapter of the Qur'an titled "Maryam" (Surah
19). This chapter recounts the angel Gabriel's visit to Mary, during
which he announced that she would conceive and give birth to Jesus.

> And mention in the Book (the Qur'an, O Muhammad
> صلى الله عليه وسلم the story of) Maryam (Mary), when she
> withdrew in seclusion from her family to a place facing
> east.

> She placed a screen (to screen herself) from them; then
> We sent to her Our Ruh [angel Jibril (Gabriel)], and he
> appeared before her in the form of a man in all respects.

> She said: "Verily! I seek refuge with the Most Gracious
> (Allah) from you, if you do fear Allah."

> (The angel) said: "I am only a messenger from your Lord,
> (to announce) to you the gift of a righteous son" (Surah
> 19:16-19).

In the biblical account (Luke 1:34), Mary questioned Gabriel,
asking how this would be possible, for she was a virgin. Gabriel
said that her conception and virgin birth would be miracles carried
out by God Himself. The Qur'an mentions a conversation between
Mary and Gabriel as well, with these details:

> She said: "How can I have a son, when no man has
> touched me, nor am I unchaste?"

> He said: "So (it will be), your Lord said: 'That is easy for
> Me (Allah): And (We wish) to appoint him as a sign to
> mankind and a mercy from Us (Allah), and it is a mat-
> ter (already) decreed, (by Allah).'"

> So she conceived him, and she withdrew with him to
> a far place (i.e. Bethlehem valley about 4-6 miles from
> Jerusalem).

> And the pains of childbirth drove her to the trunk of a
> date-palm. She said: "Would that I had died before this,
> and had been forgotten and out of sight!"

> Then [the babe 'Îsa (Jesus) or Jibril (Gabriel)] cried unto
> her from below her, saying: "Grieve not: your Lord has
> provided a water stream under you.

> "And shake the trunk of date-palm towards you, it will let
> fall fresh ripe-dates upon you."

"So eat and drink and be glad. And if you see any human being, say: 'Verily! I have vowed a fast unto the Most Gracious (Allah) so I shall not speak to any human being this day.'"

Then she brought him (the baby) to her people, carrying him. They said: "O Mary! Indeed you have brought a thing Fariyy (a mighty thing)" [Tafsir Al-Tabari] (Surah 19:20-27).

THE VIRGIN MARY, OR MIRIAM THE SISTER OF MOSES?

Critics have noted that the Qur'an appears to confuse Mary the mother of Jesus in the New Testament with Miriam of the Old Testament, who was the sister of Aaron and lived some 1,400 years earlier. For example, in the Qur'an, the name of Mary's father is Imran. "And Maryam (Mary), the daughter of 'Imran who guarded her chastity…'" (Surah 66:12). Imran sounds very similar to the biblical name Amram, who was the father of Miriam, Moses, and Aaron (Exodus 6:20; 15:20).

This mistake seems to be confirmed when the Qur'an calls Jesus's mother, Mary, the sister of Aaron shortly before the newborn Jesus is said to speak from His cradle. In the Maryam chapter, immediately following the birth of Jesus, the Qur'an states:

"O sister (i.e. the like) of Harun (Aaron)! Your father was not a man who used to commit adultery, nor your mother was an unchaste woman."

Then she pointed to him. They said: "How can we talk to one who is a child in the cradle?"

"He ['Îsa (Jesus)] said: "Verily I am a slave of Allah, He has given me the Scripture and made me a Prophet…"

Such is 'Îsa (Jesus), son of Maryam (Mary). (It is) a

statement of truth, about which they doubt (or dispute) (Surah 19:28-30,34).

Muslim apologists, in various ways, have attempted to harmonize this apparent conflating of the Old Testament Miriam with the first century Maryam, the mother of Jesus.[1] Nevertheless, it is remarkable that Jesus is presented in the Qur'an as the only prophet who was miraculously born of a virgin. No other prophet in Islam, including Muhammad, is said to be virgin born.

For Christians, the virgin birth of Jesus has tremendous implications on His identity. The virgin birth gives Christians further evidence that Jesus was more than a mere prophet. He was both the Son of Man and uniquely the Son of God. Christians cite Matthew chapter 1 as evidence that the virgin birth was a fulfillment of Isaiah's prophecy that "a virgin will conceive and bear a son" who would be "Immanuel" (Isaiah 7:14)—that is, "God with us."

> Now the birth of Jesus Christ was as follows: when His mother Mary had been betrothed to Joseph, before they came together she was found to be with child by the Holy Spirit And Joseph her husband, being a righteous man and not wanting to disgrace her, planned to send her away secretly. But when he had considered this, behold, an angel of the Lord appeared to him in a dream, saying, "Joseph, son of David, do not be afraid to take Mary as your wife; for the Child who has been conceived in her is of the Holy Spirit. She will bear a Son; and you shall call His name Jesus, for He will save His people from their sins." Now all this took place to fulfill what was spoken by the Lord through the prophet: "Behold, the virgin shall be with child and shall bear a Son, and they shall call His name Immanuel," which translated means, "God with us." And Joseph awoke from his sleep and did as the angel of the Lord commanded him, and took Mary as his wife, but kept her a virgin until she

gave birth to a Son; and he called His name Jesus (Matthew 1:18-25).

The Qur'an, however, does not teach that the virgin birth of Jesus is evidence that He was deity or the Son of God. In fact, in context, the Qur'an teaches the opposite. As we will see later in this book, the Qur'an presents Jesus as "a Word from God"—as a created being, and not the Creator.

In the Qur'an, when Mary asked how she could conceive and have a son, this is the answer that was given:

> She said: "O my Lord! How shall I have a son when no man has touched me." He said: "So (it will be) for Allah creates what He wills. When He has decreed something, He says to it only: 'Be!'—and it is.
>
> And He (Allah) will teach him [('Îsa (Jesus)] the Book and Al-Hikmah (i.e. the Sunnah, the faultless speech of the Prophets, wisdom), (and) the Taurat (Torah) and the Injeel (Gospel)" (Surah 3:47-48).

Thus, the Qur'an teaches that Jesus was the son of the virgin Mary (*'Îsa ibn Maryam*), but adamantly denies that Jesus is deity.

------- **QUESTIONS FOR DISCUSSION** -------

Muslims see Jesus as a created being, and not the Creator of all things. His virgin birth is not seen as evidence for divinity, but as a sign pointing to a miracle from Allah. The birth of Jesus is viewed as a miraculous event similar to Allah's creation of Adam.

Nevertheless, the birth of Jesus was unique, according to Qur'an. No other human is said to be virgin born, and no other prophet, including Muhammad, was born in this fashion. The Qur'an and the Bible both teach that Jesus was born of a virgin, but they come to very different conclusions about the implications of that fact. Here are some questions for Muslims that may help clarify some of those similarities and the differences:

- Does the Qur'an teach that Jesus was born of a virgin?

- According to the Qur'an, was any other teacher or prophet born of a virgin besides Jesus?

- Can I share with you why Christians believe that the virgin birth of Jesus is a sign that Jesus was more than just a prophet?

Chapter 5

Jesus of the Qur'an Is "the Word"

The Christian idea of the logos *is completely different from the simple Islamic understanding of the "Word."...Jesus was a "Word" from God.*

IMAM KAMIL MUFTI, MUSLIM SCHOLAR
(The Religion of Islam[1])

Another striking parallel between the New Testament and the Qur'an is use of the title "Word of God" for Jesus. As is true about other words and phrases, however, it is essential to realize that Christians and Muslims mean very different things by this title.

JESUS AS "THE WORD"

The New Testament Gospel of John refers to Jesus as "the Word" (Greek, *ho logos*)." Thus in John 1, Jesus, "the Word," is presented not as a creature Himself, but as being the creator of "all things" in the beginning.

> In the beginning was the Word, and the Word was with God, and the Word was God. He was in the beginning with God. All things came into being through Him, and apart from Him nothing came into being that has come into being (John 1:1-3).

The Qur'an also applies the title "Word of God" to Jesus. For example, the Qur'an quotes angels telling Mary that her son would be called a "Word from Him (God)" (Surah 3:45).

> The Angels said, "O Mary, God gives you good news of a Word from Him. His name is the Messiah, Jesus, son of Mary, well-esteemed in this world and the next, and one of the nearest (Surah 3:45; *ClearQuran,* Talal Itani translation).

This is significant, as noted by one prominent Muslim website, The Religion of Islam. Here, Imam Kamil Mufti writes, "Jesus is referred to as a 'Word' from God in three passages in the Quran. No other prophet has been described with such a title."[2]

Unlike the Bible, however, the Qur'an never associates the title "Word of God" with the deity of Jesus. Instead, the Qur'an insists that as "His Word," Jesus could in no way be either the Creator or God. In fact, the Qur'an goes so far as to teach the opposite. Christians in particular are warned not to "exceed the limits in your religion" by calling "His Word" God, the Son of God, or one of three persons of the Trinity. Jesus, the Qur'an insists, must be seen as "no more than" a prophet:

> O people of the Scripture (Christians)! Do not exceed the limits in your religion, nor say of Allah aught but the truth. The Messiah 'Îsa (Jesus), son of Maryam (Mary), was (no more than) a Messenger of Allah and His Word, ("Be!"—and he was) which He bestowed on Maryam (Mary) and a spirit (Ruh) created by Him; so believe in Allah and His Messengers. Say not: "Three (trinity)!" Cease! (it is) better for you. For Allah is (the only) One Ilah (God), glory be to Him (Far Exalted is He) above having a son. To Him belongs all that is in the heavens and all that is in the earth. And Allah is All-Sufficient as a Disposer of affairs (Surah 4:171).

The popular Muslim apologist and debater Shabir Ally explains the Muslim understanding of "Word of God" and attempts to apply that meaning to John's Gospel and Paul's epistles in the New Testament:

> This Gospel in its final form says one more thing about Jesus that was unknown from the previous three Gospels—that Jesus was the Word of God. John means that Jesus was God's agent through whom God created everything else. This is often misunderstood to mean that Jesus was God Himself. But John was saying, as Paul had already said, that Jesus was God's first creature.[3]

It is hard to justify that interpretation with John's Gospel when considering the context. As we have already seen, John not only called Jesus "the Word," he also said "the Word was God." John also presented Jesus as the Creator and not a creature, saying that "all things" were created "through Him." The apostle Paul also identified Jesus as the Creator of all things, saying that Jesus was "the image of the invisible God the firstborn of all creation" (Colossians 1:15). The word "firstborn" (Greek, *prōtotokos*) here means "preeminent."[4] Paul did not mean that Jesus was the firstborn man—that would have been Cain (Genesis 4:1). Nor did Paul mean that Jesus was one of the created beings. The next verse explains:

> By Him all things were created, both in the heavens and on earth, visible and invisible, whether thrones or dominions or rulers or authorities—all things have been created through Him and for Him (verse 16).

If Paul taught that Jesus created *all* things visible and invisible, it is hard to imagine that Paul meant that Jesus created Himself. When the Bible speaks of God creating the heavens and earth, it describes a sovereign act demonstrating omnipotence. God is not pictured as needing an intermediate agent of creation or some assistant or subcontractor. God required no intermediate, no angel, no prophet to assist Him in the work of creation.

> Thus says the LORD, your Redeemer, and the one who formed you from the womb, "I, the LORD, am the maker of all things, stretching out the heavens by Myself and spreading out the earth all alone" (Isaiah 44:24).

────── **QUESTIONS FOR DISCUSSION** ──────

The Qur'an presents Jesus as "His Word," as a created being whom God spoke into being by saying "('Be!'—and he was)" (Surah 4:171). In contrast, the Bible teaches that by Himself, God created all things visible and invisible through a sovereign and omnipotent act of His will through "the word" (Hebrews 11:3). Jesus is identified as "the Word" who not only was "with God" in the beginning, but also "the Word was God" Himself (John 1:1). Finally, "the Word" (Jesus) is honored in Scripture for creating all things that have been created (John 1:3; Colossians 1:15-16).

- The Qur'an teaches that Jesus was a "Word of God." What does that title mean to you?

- Do you believe that God created all things by Himself? Or did He use or need help? What does Isaiah 44:24 say?

- The Christian Scriptures teach that Jesus was the "Word of God," but the meaning here is different than that given in the Qur'an. Based on John 1:1-3 and Colossians 1:15-16, what does "the Word of God" mean to Christians?

Chapter 6

Jesus of the Qur'an
Is Called "the Messiah"

*...the Quran agrees with the Christians who identify Jesus
to be the Messiah, but considers their insistence that
the Messiah is the son of God to be blasphemy.*

IMAM KAMIL MUFTI, MUSLIM SCHOLAR
(The Religion of Islam[1])

According to Jewish expectations, the coming Messiah would rescue the people of God by overthrowing the unrighteous government that ruled over them, addressing injustice, and establishing a golden age of peace and well-being under God's rule.

JESUS AS "MESSIAH"

The title *Messiah* or *Christ* means "anointed one," and is used throughout the New Testament to identify Jesus as the fulfillment of the Old Testament promises of the righteous "Branch" to come (Isaiah 4:2). This Messiah will "take away our reproach" (verse 1), and being the righteous judge, he "will again recover the second time with His hand the remnant of His people" (Isaiah 11:11).

> He found first his own brother Simon and said to him,
> "We have found the Messiah [Greek, *Messías*]" (which
> translated means Christ [Greek, *Christós*]) (John 1:41).

Both the Hebrew word for Messiah, *māšiyah*, and the corresponding Greek word, *christós*, literally mean "anointed" or "anointed one." In the Old Testament, priests and kings of Israel were anointed with oil during their commissioning ceremony. For example, the prophet Samuel anointed David with oil, identifying him as the future king of Israel (1 Samuel 16:12-13).

Even the Persian king Cyrus was referred to as God's "messiah" or "anointed" in Isaiah 45:1. Although he was not *the* Messiah, he temporarily functioned as a type of "shepherd" of God (Isaiah 44:28), enacting God's redemption for Israel by decreeing that Jerusalem be rebuilt, which allowed for the reconstruction of the temple.

Eventually, God's prophesied anointed one was thought to be a shepherd and redeemer who would sit on the throne of David, restoring the people of God politically and spiritually.

In the New Testament, the concept of the promised Messiah or anointed one was directly tied to redemption and salvation for God's people. Luke recorded the words of the angel who announced the birth of Jesus to the shepherds:

> The angel said to them, "Do not be afraid; for behold, I bring you good news of great joy which will be for all the people; for today in the city of David there has been born for you a Savior, who is Christ the Lord" (Luke 2:10-11).

Christians are often surprised to find that the Qur'an also uses the title *Messiah* in reference to Jesus. Imam Kamil Mufti states, "The Quran refers to Jesus as the Messiah (*al-Maseeh*) at least nine times [3:45; 4:157,171-172; 5:17,72,75; 9:30-31]."[2] For example, the Qur'an teaches:

> (Remember) when the angels said: "O Maryam (Mary)! Verily, Allah gives you the glad tidings of a Word ["Be!"— and he was! i.e. 'Îsa (Jesus) the son of Maryam (Mary)]

from Him, his name will be the Messiah 'Îsa (Jesus), the son of Maryam (Mary), held in honour in this world and in the Hereafter, and will be one of those who are near to Allah" (Surah 3:45).

It is important to know that Muslims' understanding of the term "Messiah," as used in the Qur'an, is radically different than that of either Jews or Christians. There is little tolerance for the Christian concept of a Messiah/Savior in Islam—especially among Sunni Muslims.

> Some claim that the idea of Messianism is not Islamic. *The New Encyclopaedia Britannica* says that "Islam is not a Messianic religion and has no room for a Saviour-Messiah." Riffat Hasan supports this thesis and states that: "Messianism appears to be incompatible with the teachings of the Qur'an, nonetheless...Messianism is an essential part of religious belief and practice for almost all Shi'a Muslims. Shi'a Messianism does not fit theologically or logically into the framework of normative Islam."[3]

While referring to Jesus as "the Messiah," the Qur'an clearly teaches that the title does not make Him any different from God's other prophets or messengers:

> The Messiah ['Îsa (Jesus)], son of Maryam (Mary), was no more than a Messenger; many were the Messengers that passed away before him. His mother [Maryam (Mary)] was a Siddiqah [i.e. she believed in the Words of Allah and His Books (see Verse 66:12)]. They both used to eat food (as any other human being, while Allah does not eat). Look how We make the Ayat (proofs, evidence, verses, lessons, signs, revelations, etc.) clear to them; yet look how they are deluded away (from the truth) (Surah 5:75).

Thus, the term "Messiah," as used in the Qur'an, cannot be cited as evidence that Islam teaches that Jesus is the Savior of the world or the Son of God. The Qur'an clearly criticizes these doctrines as Christian heresies that ultimately bring Allah's curse upon those who believe them.

> And the Jews say: "Uzair (Ezra) is the son of Allah, and the Christians say: Messiah is the son of Allah. That is their saying with their mouths, resembling the saying of those who disbelieved aforetime. Allah's Curse be on them, how they are deluded away from the truth!" (Surah 9:30).

——— **QUESTIONS FOR DISCUSSION** ———

While both the New Testament and the Qur'an refer to Jesus as the Messiah, Christians and Muslims attach very different meanings to the term. With these important distinctions in mind, here are some questions to help facilitate a gospel discussion with Muslims.

- Does the Qur'an teach that Jesus was the Messiah?

- What does the title *Messiah* mean to a Muslim?

- Christians also believe that Jesus was the Messiah. Can I show you a passage in the Gospels (Luke 2:10-11) that explains what we mean by the term *Messiah*?

Chapter 7

Jesus of the Qur'an Performed Miracles

Jesus raised the dead. He healed the sick. But He did not do
it in His own power or authority. He was only a prophet, a
messenger. Everything He did was done through Him by Allah.

ELIJAH, FORMER SHIA MUSLIM
(Interview—see chapter 18)

The Qur'an affirms that Jesus performed miraculous signs as proof that He was a prophet of God. These include several miracles that are also recorded in the New Testament Gospels, such as Jesus healing a leper, a person born blind, and raising the dead. For example, the Qur'an quotes Jesus as saying, "I heal him who was born blind, and the leper, and I bring the dead to life by Allah's Leave" (Surah 3:49).

Also, as discussed earlier, the Qur'an describes the miraculous virgin birth of Jesus as a supernatural act of God that serves as a clear sign confirming Jesus's divine calling as God's messenger:

> She said: "How can I have a son, when no man has touched me, nor am I unchaste?"
>
> He said: "So (it will be), your Lord said: 'That is easy for Me (Allah): And (We wish) to appoint him as a sign to mankind and a mercy from Us (Allah), and it is a matter (already) decreed, (by Allah)'" (Surah 19:20-21).

The Qur'an also lists several miracles not documented in the

Bible. In Surah 5, the disciples asked Jesus for a banquet of heavenly food to be sent from the presence of God.

> (Remember) when Al-Hawariyyun (the disciples) said: "O 'Isa (Jesus), son of Maryam (Mary)! Can your Lord send down to us a table spread (with food) from heaven?" 'Isa (Jesus) said: "Fear Allah, if you are indeed believers."
>
> They said: "We wish to eat thereof and to satisfy our hearts (to be stronger in Faith), and to know that you have indeed told us the truth and that we ourselves be its witnesses."
>
> 'Isa (Jesus), son of Maryam (Mary), said: "O Allah, our Lord! Send us from the heaven a table spread (with food) that there may be for us—for the first and the last of us—a festival and a sign from You; and provide us sustenance, for You are the Best of sustainers."
>
> Allah said: "I am going to send it down unto you..." (Surah 5:112-115).

Another extrabiblical miracle found in the Qur'an is that of the baby Jesus speaking from the cradle at birth. This miracle was prophesied in Surah 3:46 and fulfilled, as cited earlier, in the chapter devoted to Maryam (Surah 19).

> So she conceived him, and she withdrew with him to a far place (i.e. Bethlehem valley about 4-6 miles from Jerusalem).
>
> And the pains of childbirth drove her to the trunk of a date-palm. She said: "Would that I had died before this, and had been forgotten and out of sight!"
>
> Then [the babe 'Isa (Jesus) or Jibril (Gabriel)] cried unto her from below her, saying: "Grieve not: your Lord has provided a water stream under you.

"And shake the trunk of date-palm towards you, it will let fall fresh ripe-dates upon you."

"So eat and drink and be glad. And if you see any human being, say: 'Verily! I have vowed a fast unto the Most Gracious (Allah) so I shall not speak to any human being this day'" (Surah 19:22-26).

There is a question among some Muslims about whether it was Jesus or the angel Gabriel who spoke in this initial passage. It is very clear in the verses that follow, however, that it is the newborn baby Jesus speaking theological doctrines from the cradle.

Then she brought him (the baby) to her people, carrying him. They said: "O Mary! Indeed you have brought a thing Fariyy (a mighty thing) [Tafsir Al-Tabari].

"O sister (i.e. the like) of Harun (Aaron)! Your father was not a man who used to commit adultery, nor your mother was an unchaste woman."

Then she pointed to him. They said: "How can we talk to one who is a child in the cradle?"

"He ['Îsa (Jesus)] said: "Verily I am a slave of Allah, He has given me the Scripture and made me a Prophet;"

"And He has made me blessed wheresoever I be, and has enjoined on me Salat (prayer), and Zakat, as long as I live."

"And dutiful to my mother, and made me not arrogant, unblest.

"And Salam (peace) be upon me the day I was born, and the day I die, and the day I shall be raised alive!"

Such is 'Îsa (Jesus), son of Maryam (Mary). (It is) a statement of truth, about which they doubt (or dispute) (Surah 19:27-34).

Another example of an extrabiblical miracle is the account of Jesus breathing life into a clay bird.

> And will make him ['Īsa (Jesus)] a Messenger to the Children of Israel (saying): "I have come to you with a sign from your Lord, that I design for you out of clay, a figure like that of a bird, and breathe into it…Surely, therein is a sign for you, if you believe" (Surah 3:49).

Critics of the Qur'an have suggested that Muhammad may have borrowed some of these miracle stories from earlier sources.[1] Nevertheless, it is significant that the Qur'an presents Jesus as a prophet of God confirmed by numerous miracles and powerful signs from God.

It is interesting to contrast the miracles of Jesus in the Qur'an with those of Muhammad. The Qur'an does not attribute to Muhammad any miracles like those done by Jesus, such as healing the blind or raising the dead. The Hadith contains numerous accounts of miracles performed by Muhammad, but these were compiled centuries after his death. The Qur'an itself mentions virtually no miracles done by Muhammad.[2]

Muslims often point to the Qur'an itself as the greatest miracle of Muhammad. They believe that the literary style and linguistic beauty of the Arabic Qur'an would be impossible to produce without divine help. The Qur'an itself challenges doubters to reproduce something similar, implying that it would be impossible to produce even one chapter that would be equivalent (Surah 2:23).[3]

The Arabic word *ayah,* often translated "miracle" in the Qur'an, may also be translated as "sign." It is also the same Arabic word used for the "verses" found within the surahs (chapters) of the Qur'an. Thus, because there are 6,236 verses in the Qur'an, Muslims argue that Muhammad performed 6,236 miracles.

——————— QUESTIONS FOR DISCUSSION ———————

The Qur'an teaches that Jesus performed many miracles, such as healing the sick, giving sight to the blind, and raising the dead. These miracles, or signs, were presented as proof that Jesus was sent by God.

The New Testament Gospels also record many miracles done by Jesus. In the biblical accounts, these miracles are cited as evidence of a much different identity and ministry. For example, in John's Gospel, the signs and miracles were documented for the specific purpose of identifying Jesus as the Son of God, the Savior who gives eternal life to those who believe on His name:

> Many other signs [or attesting miracles] Jesus also performed in the presence of the disciples, which are not written in this book; but these have been written so that you may believe that Jesus is the Christ, the Son of God; and that believing you may have life in His name (John 20:30-31).

No other prophet in the Bible or Qur'an performed miracles of this scope and magnitude. The significance of this may be explored in the following questions:

- Does the Qur'an teach that Jesus performed miracles as a sign or proof that He was sent by God? What are some examples?

- What miracles of Jesus found in the Qur'an can also be verified by accounts in the New Testament Gospels?

- John, in his Gospel, wrote that the miracles he recorded were selected for a specific purpose. Would you like to see what that purpose was, according to John 20:30-31?

Chapter 8

Jesus of the Qur'an Will Return Again in the End Times

...Jesus did not die but was raised to the presence of Allah...
Jesus will come back to earth towards the end of time...

HARUN YAHYA, MUSLIM SCHOLAR
(IslamiCity.org[1])

Like Christians, Muslims believe that Jesus will return to Earth during the end times. There is, however, virtually nothing explicit in the Qur'an itself about the return of Jesus. There are at best only a few vague statements that Muslims generally interpret as references to an earthly return of Jesus. For example, in Surah 43, Jesus is cryptically identified as being a "sign for the Hour." Muslims believe that phrase is a code word of some kind that prophesies a return or coming of Jesus in the last days.

> And he ['Îsa (Jesus), son of Maryam (Mary)] shall be
> a known sign for (the coming of) the Hour (Day of
> Resurrection) [i.e. 'Îsa's (Jesus) descent on the earth].
> Therefore have no doubt concerning it (i.e. the Day of
> Resurrection). And follow Me (Allah) (i.e. be obedient
> to Allah and do what He orders you to do, O mankind)!
> This is the Straight Path (of Islamic Monotheism, lead-
> ing to Allah and to His Paradise) (Surah 43:61).

As seen in the parenthetic additions in the verse above, some translators, as well as Quranic interpreters known as *mufassirs,* supplement the text of the Qur'an with further clarifications. Here, they interpret the Arabic word translated "sign for" to mean "coming of" and "the Hour" as a reference to the "Day of Resurrection." This "Day of Resurrection" does not pertain to the bodily resurrection of Jesus after the crucifixion, as both of these events are firmly denied by Muslims. Rather, this supplement is prophesying an end-time event that will include Jesus's "descent on the earth." With the additional wording, this passage does seem to reference some type of return of Jesus in the future. However, the supplement also adds a great deal of new information to the passage, including specifics clearly not found in the verse itself.

The primary sources of Islamic teachings about the end times, including those related to Jesus's return, are found not in the Qur'an, but in the Hadith, which contains much more detailed information. For instance, in Hadith that are considered by Muslims to be highly reliable, we find the following words in connection with Surah 4:159:

> Allah's Messenger said, "By Him in Whose Hands my soul is, surely (Jesus,) the son of Mary will soon descend amongst you and will judge mankind justly (as a Just Ruler); he will break the Cross and kill the pigs and there will be no Jizya (i.e. taxation taken from non-Muslims). Money will be in abundance so that nobody will accept it, and a single prostration to Allah (in prayer) will be better than the whole world and whatever is in it." Abu Huraira added "If you wish, you can recite (this verse of the Holy Book):—'And there is none Of the people of the Scriptures (Jews and Christians) But must believe in him (i.e Jesus as an Apostle of Allah and a human being) Before his death. And on the Day of Judgment He will be a witness Against them'" (Sahih Bukhari: Book 60, Hadith 118—Narrated Abu Huraira).[2]

More specifically, in Book 37 of Sunan Abu-Dawud, there is found a description of what Jesus will look like, including His hair color and clothing, so that people will recognize Him. However, this passage does not say Jesus is returning to reign forever, as taught in the Bible (Revelation 11:15). Instead, it says Jesus is coming back to kill the Antichrist (*Al-Masih ad-Dajjal*), destroy all non-Muslim religions, live for 40 years, and then die.

> The Prophet (peace be upon him) said: There is no prophet between me and him, that is, Jesus (peace be upon him). He will descent [sic] (to the earth). When you see him, recognise him: a man of medium height, reddish hair, wearing two light yellow garments, looking as if drops were falling down from his head though it will not be wet. He will fight the people for the cause of Islam. He will break the cross, kill swine, and abolish jizyah [tax imposed on non-Muslims]. Allah will perish all religions except Islam. He will destroy the Antichrist and will live on the earth for forty years and then he will die. The Muslims will pray over him (Sunan Abu-Dawud: Book 37, Number 4310—Narrated Abu Huraira).[3]

Sunni and Shia[4] Muslims have different understandings of what will transpire in the end times. While the details vary, Muslims agree that the last days will be marked by corruption and wickedness. Jesus will descend back to Earth to help rescue God's people from tyranny, destroy evil, eliminate false religions, and restore pure Islam.

──────── **QUESTIONS FOR DISCUSSION** ────────

The New Testament records the ascension of Jesus to heaven and places it after His crucifixion, death, bodily resurrection, and 40-day ministry among His disciples and others. The Bible provides an eyewitness account of Jesus ascending into the clouds from the Mount of Olives outside of Jerusalem, accompanied by angelic confirmation of His second coming:

> After He had said these things, He was lifted up while they were looking on, and a cloud received Him out of their sight. And as they were gazing intently into the sky while He was going, behold, two men in white clothing stood beside them. They also said, "Men of Galilee, why do you stand looking into the sky? This Jesus, who has been taken up from you into heaven, will come in just the same way as you have watched Him go into heaven" (Acts 1:9-11).

The Bible teaches that at the first coming of Jesus, His death was a sacrificial offering to pay for the sins of His people. He will return visibly in judgment to reign over all the earth. The second time He appears, it will be for those He has redeemed, those who eagerly await His return.

> Christ also, having been offered once to bear the sins of many, will appear a second time for salvation without reference to sin, to those who eagerly await Him (Hebrews 9:28).

The Bible describes this as the "blessed hope" marked by the "appearing of the glory of our great God and Savior, Jesus Christ" (Titus 2:13-14). Christians await Jesus's return with great anticipation, for it is at that time that He will usher in His perfect kingdom, and they will be given new bodies no longer impaired by sin.

- Do Muslims believe that Jesus will return to Earth one day?

- What do you believe Jesus will do when He returns to earth?

- Christians look forward to the appearance of Jesus. Can I tell you why we call that our "blessed hope"?

Chapter 9

Jesus of the Qur'an Is "Another Jesus"

Verily, the likeness of 'Īsa (Jesus) before Allah is the
likeness of Adam. He created him from dust, then
(He) said to him: "Be!"—and he was.

Qur'an, Surah 3:59

As mentioned in the previous chapters, there are some interesting parallels between the Jesus depicted in the Qur'an and the Jesus presented in the Bible. For Christians, these similarities can serve as great catalysts for discussions with Muslim friends and coworkers. Muslims have a deep respect for Jesus and generally enjoy talking about Him. These conversations can be used as springboards to transition into productive dialogues about the biblical Jesus and the gospel of grace.

In their discussions, Christians should be careful not to assume that the Jesus of the Qur'an is the same Jesus followed by Christians. Even when the Qur'an and Bible use similar-sounding titles and descriptions such as *Messiah, Word of God,* and *virgin birth,* these terms have radically different definitions and interpretations for the two religious groups. It could be said that Muslims and Christians often use the same vocabulary, but with different dictionaries.

To avoid misunderstandings, Muslims and Christians should both take great care to define their terms. They should always be clear to communicate what they mean, as well as what they *do not* mean.

ANOTHER JESUS?

Even in the first century AD, the apostle Paul warned of those who would preach "another Jesus" not proclaimed by the apostles and legitimate Christian churches. This other Jesus calls into question the source of their teachings ("a different spirit") and the content of their salvation message ("a different gospel").

> I am afraid that, as the serpent deceived Eve by his craftiness, your minds will be led astray from the simplicity and purity of devotion to Christ. For if one comes and preaches another Jesus whom we have not preached, or you receive a different spirit which you have not received, or a different gospel which you have not accepted, you bear this beautifully (2 Corinthians 11:3-4).

ANOTHER GOD?

Fundamental to the controversy of "another Jesus" is the question of the identity of God. Do Muslims and Christians worship the same God? Again, we find many similarities. Both Christianity and Islam are monotheistic religions that believe in only one true God. Both religions, along with Judaism, look to Abraham as a father of their faith. In Arabic-language Bibles, the word *Allah* is often used to translate the Greek and Hebrew words for God in both the Old and New Testaments.[1]

There are, however, huge differences as well. The God of Islam is not a Trinity, but is only one. This doctrine is identified by the theological term *Dynamic Monarchianism*. Muslims do not believe God is one of three persons, nor do they say He is the Father of Jesus Christ. What a person believes about God will always affect what he or she believes about Jesus.

──────── **QUESTIONS FOR DISCUSSION** ────────

Despite fairly significant similarities between the Jesus of the Qur'an and the Jesus of the Bible, the differences are overwhelming. The Qur'an seems to go out of its way to deny, contradict, or even condemn virtually all the essential elements of Jesus's identity and ministry as found in the New Testament and believed by Christians.

The upcoming chapters will explore some of those major differences, which are crucial because they mean the difference between eternal life in heaven or eternal condemnation in hell. In the Bible, Jesus said,

> I said to you that you will die in your sins; for unless you believe that I am He [see Exodus 3:13-14], you will die in your sins (John 8:24).

- If Christians and Muslims both believe in one true God, does that mean that they are both worshipping the same God?

- Is the identity of Jesus in the Qur'an identical with the identity of Jesus in the New Testament?

- What are some of the similarities and differences?

- According to the Bible, why is it important that we know the true identity of Jesus?

Chapter 10

Jesus of the Qur'an Is
Not the Son of God

…the Qur'an…clearly denies that Jesus Christ was the Son of God.

Zia Hassan, former Muslim
(Interview—see chapter 17)

The Qur'an insists that Jesus is a prophet of God, but is not the Son of God. This is perhaps the first major difference one notices between the Christian and Islamic concepts of Jesus. All four New Testament Gospels clearly identify Jesus as the Son of God.

Mark's Gospel begins with the affirmation, "The beginning of the gospel of Jesus Christ, the Son of God" (Mark 1:1). Jesus calls Himself "the Son of God" in Luke 22:70. John the Baptist testifies that "this is the Son of God" (John 1:34). Even the devil (Matthew 4:3-6; Luke 4:3-9) and demons acknowledge that Jesus is the "Son of God" (Matthew 8:29; Mark 3:11; Luke 4:3,41).

John's Gospel was written for the very purpose that those who read it would believe that Jesus is the Son of God and have salvation through that belief.

> Many other signs Jesus also performed in the presence of the disciples, which are not written in this book; but these have been written so that you may believe that Jesus is the Christ, the Son of God; and that believing you may have life in His name (John 20:30-31).

This is also confirmed by the angel Gabriel, who announced to the virgin Mary that her child would be identified as "the Son of God." It should be noted that this is the same angel Gabriel who was said to have recited the Qur'an to Muhammad.

> The angel [Gabriel] answered and said to her, "The Holy Spirit will come upon you, and the power of the Most High will overshadow you; and for that reason the holy Child shall be called the Son of God" (Luke 1:35).

The Qur'an, however, is adamant that Jesus is not the Son of God. It is impossible for God to either have a son or be a son because, according to Islam, "He begets not, nor was He begotten."

> Say (O Muhammad): "He is Allah, (the) One.
>
> "Allah-us-Samad [Allah the Self-Sufficient Master, Whom all creatures need, (He neither eats nor drinks)].
>
> "He begets not, nor was He begotten.
>
> "And there is none co-equal or comparable unto Him" (Surah 112:1-4).

Jesus, in Muslim theology, is revered as a prophet beloved of Allah who was miraculously born of a virgin. According to the Qur'an, however, that does not suggest in any way that Jesus could be called the Son of God. He is the son of Maryam (Mary) only. Thus, Jesus was miraculously created by the Word of Allah "Be!—and it is" in a similar way that the first man, Adam, was a special creation of God without being the Son of God.

> Such is 'Îsa (Jesus), son of Maryam (Mary). (It is) a statement of truth, about which they doubt (or dispute).
>
> It befits not (the Majesty of) Allah that He should beget a son [this refers to the slander of Christians against Allah, by saying that 'Îsa (Jesus) is the son of Allah].

Glorified (and Exalted) be He (above all that they associate with Him). When He decrees a thing, He only says to it: "Be!"—and it is.

['Îsa (Jesus) said]: "And verily Allah is my Lord and your Lord. So worship Him (Alone). That is the Straight Path. (Allah's religion of Islamic Monotheism which He did ordain for all of His Prophets)" [Tafsir At-Tabari] (Surah 19:34-36).

The Qur'an acknowledges that Christians affirm that Jesus is the Son of God, but condemns them for such heresy, accusing them of slandering God when they do this. On the Day of Judgment, those Christians who affirm Jesus as the Son of God are at risk of being condemned to the fires of hell.

Then the sects differed [i.e. the Christians about 'Îsa (Jesus) عليه السلام], so woe unto the disbelievers [those who gave false witness by saying that 'Îsa (Jesus) is the son of Allah] from the Meeting of a great Day (i.e. the Day of Resurrection, when they will be thrown in the blazing Fire).

How clearly will they (polytheists and disbelievers in the Oneness of Allah) see and hear the Day when they will appear before Us! But the Zalimun (polytheists and wrong-doers) today are in plain error.

And warn them (O Muhammad صلى الله عليه وسلم) of the Day of grief and regrets, when the case has been decided, while (now) they are in a state of carelessness, and they believe not (Surah 19:37-39).

Affirming Jesus as the Son of God violates the essential Islamic doctrine of *tawhid,* meaning "oneness." It suggests that God has partnership with or shares His unique attributes with others—in this case, Jesus. This violation of oneness is described as the sin of *shirk* (association), which, apart from repentance, may be regarded as an unpardonable sin in Islam. Indeed, Allah may forgive other sins, but this sin of shirk (ascribing association or partnership between Allah and any other) "Allah forgives not."

> Verily, Allah forgives not that partners should be set up with Him (in worship), but He forgives except that (anything else) to whom He wills; and whoever sets up partners with Allah in worship, he has indeed invented a tremendous sin.

> Have you not seen those (Jews and Christians) who claim sanctity for themselves. Nay, but Allah sanctifies whom He wills, and they will not be dealt with injustice even equal to the extent of a scalish thread in the long slit of a date-stone (Surah 4:48-49).

Christians agree that by referring to Himself as the unique Son of God, Jesus was making divine claims. The Jews who heard Jesus make these claims came to similar conclusions and wanted to kill Jesus for it. Jesus responded that He does nothing independently or out of harmony with the works of God. He said that whatever God the Father does, the Son does as well. No mere human could truthfully state that he can do the works of God.

> For this reason therefore the Jews were seeking all the more to kill Him, because He not only was breaking the Sabbath, but also was calling God His own Father, making Himself equal with God. Therefore Jesus answered and was saying to them, "Truly, truly, I say to you, the Son can do nothing of Himself, unless it is something He sees the Father doing; for whatever the Father does, these things the Son also does in like manner (John 5:18-19).

The Islamic problem with Jesus taking the title Son of God is magnified by the tendency for Muslims to equate "Son of God" with the blasphemous idea that God had sexual relations with Mary to produce Jesus. Of course, this has never been the Christian meaning of that title. Joseph Cumming, pastor of the International Church at Yale University, notes:

> But most Muslims do find deeply offensive…the assertion that Jesus Christ is the "Son of God." In my 15 years living in an Islamic Republic in the Arab world, and my additional 12 years working daily with Muslims in the U.S. and around the world, I have found that many Muslims consider this Christian belief to be more offensive than any other…
>
> [W]hen a Christian says, "I believe Jesus is the Son of God," often what the Christian's Muslim friend hears is: "I believe God had sexual relations with Mary and carnally produced an illegitimate divine-human offspring."[1]

This common misunderstanding has motivated some Christian missionaries and Bible translators to replace the New Testament phrase "Son of God" with other terminology that is less likely to be misinterpreted by or offend Muslim readers. A recent *Christianity Today* article noted:

> In some Bible translations, the language of Jesus' relationship to God the Father (e.g. "Son of God") is softened to stem confusion and anger from Muslims who mistakenly believe this means that God engaged in sexual relations with Mary.[2]

While misinterpretation and misunderstanding should never be the desired outcome of Christian missionaries or Bible translations, replacing biblical titles like "Son of God" with less offensive terms is not the answer. Rather than correcting the misunderstanding, replacing "Son" with "representative" or "Son of God" with

"Caliph of Allah" in "Islamic friendly"[3] Bible translations creates its own set of problems. Muslim scholars can easily discover the meaning of the New Testament Greek phrase υἱοῦ θεοῦ ["Son of God"] and end up concluding that the "people of the book" have purposely altered the Bible. Attempting to circumvent the use of "Son of God" in translations may even appear to validate the Qur'an's claim that Bible believers have corrupted or distorted their book (Surah 3:78).

This misunderstanding does, however, highlight the importance of always carefully defining terms and using care in our communications when we discuss the gospel with our Muslim friends and neighbors. It is not only essential to explain what is meant by a term, but also what is *not* meant. This is especially true when we identify Jesus as the unique Son of God.

Christians do not teach that God had a physical relationship with Mary to procreate a son. Rather, they affirm that the miracle birth of Jesus was unlike that of any other prophet. The New Testament and Christianity state that Mary was a virgin when Jesus was born (Matthew 1:20-25).

Christians also understand Jesus's Sonship to mean much more than the term *Son of God* as sometimes applied to others in different biblical contexts. In some sense, all true followers of God can be called "sons of God" metaphorically. Paul said that it is by "a spirit of adoption [that we] as sons...cry out, 'Abba! Father!'" (Romans 8:15). From the beginning of the church until today, however, the followers of Jesus have taught that Jesus is *uniquely* the Son of God. Like no other, Jesus was "with God" in the beginning, and He Himself "was God" (John 1:1).

Jesus made certain that His followers knew His true identity—that He was more than a prophet. Speaking for the disciples, Peter said this about Jesus:

> Now when Jesus came into the district of Caesarea
> Philippi, He was asking His disciples, "Who do people

say that the Son of Man is?" And they said, "Some say John the Baptist; and others, Elijah; but still others, Jeremiah, or one of the prophets." He said to them, "But who do you say that I am?" Simon Peter answered, "You are the Christ, the Son of the living God." And Jesus said to him, "Blessed are you, Simon Barjona, because flesh and blood did not reveal this to you, but My Father who is in heaven" (Matthew 16:13-17).

Peter confessed that Jesus was both "the Christ" (Messiah) and "the Son of the living God." Rather than rebuking him, Jesus affirmed Peter's declaration, saying it was a revelation from God.

—————— **QUESTIONS FOR DISCUSSION** ——————

When talking with Muslims, it is important for Christians to clarify what they mean and what they *don't* mean when they say Jesus is "the Son of God." The following questions may help facilitate that discussion:

- When Christians identify Jesus as the Son of God, what do you think is meant by that?

- May I share with you what I mean—and what I don't mean—when I say Jesus is the Son of God?

- When Muslims call Jesus the "son of Maryam [Mary]" (Surah 19:34-35), do they not also affirm that Mary was a virgin and that no procreation was involved in Jesus's birth?

- If Jesus was born of a virgin and also identified Himself as the Son of God, would this imply that He was more than a prophet?

Chapter 11

Jesus of the Qur'an Is Not the Second Person of the Trinity

When it comes to a Trinity—God the Father, the Son, the Holy Ghost, He died for our sins—this is where a Muslim and a Christian would separate and have an ocean of difference in salvation.

KHALIL MEEK, MUSLIM APOLOGIST
(Debate—see chapter 16)

The Qur'an's view of Jesus is clear: "The Messiah ['Îsa (Jesus)], son of Maryam (Mary), was no more than a Messenger" (Surah 5:75). Allah, in Islam, is not a Trinity, but a unique and absolute one. Thus, Jesus cannot be the third person of the Trinity. Besides, the Qur'an strictly condemns the concept. Before we examine what the Qur'an says, we need to know how Christians define the term *Trinity*. One could understand the Trinity as follows:

> The self-revelation of God in Scripture that His indivisible, personal essence exists eternally and necessarily as Father, Son, and Holy Spirit, and that these three are not merely nominal distinctions but personal subsistences in the divine essence.[1]

This understanding is in complete opposition to the Qur'an's teachings regarding the nature of Allah.

Arguably the most important doctrine of the Qur'an is what it teaches about the nature of Allah, which is the oneness doctrine

77

called *tawhid* (a strict form of monotheism). Understanding the place this doctrine holds among Muslims is essential to comprehending the significant differences between the Jesus of the Qur'an and the Jesus of the Bible. The focus of this Islamic doctrine is to emphasize the absolute oneness of God; the Arabic word *tawhid* means "oneness" or "unification." "Tawhid is the defining doctrine of Islam. It declares absolute monotheism—the unity and uniqueness of God as creator and sustainer of the universe."[2]

How this affects one's view of Jesus is significant. By definition, *tawhid* states that God's very nature is limited to a oneness and uniqueness that only He can have. Therefore, God can in no way have anything associated with Him. This is part of what is known as Dynamic Monarchianism, which is specifically a

> belief in the absolute unity of the God-head thereby denying the deity of the Son and the Spirit. This view teaches that the logos is an impersonal power present in all men but particularly in the man Jesus, who was an extraordinary human but not deity.[3]

The Qur'an expresses this view of God in a way that leaves no room for a God-man Jesus as portrayed throughout the New Testament. Thus, there is no Godhead; rather, there is only the singular personage of Allah. The Qur'an specifically addresses the Trinity in this way:

> O people of the Scripture (Christians)! Do not exceed the limits in your religion, nor say of Allah aught but the truth. The Messiah 'Isa (Jesus), son of Maryam (Mary), was (no more than) a Messenger of Allah and His Word, ("Be!"—and he was) which He bestowed on Maryam (Mary) and a spirit (Ruh) created by Him; so believe in Allah and His Messengers. Say not: "Three (trinity)!" Cease! (it is) better for you. For Allah is (the only) One

Ilah (God), glory be to Him (Far Exalted is He) above having a son...(Surah 4:171).

Surely, disbelievers are those who said: "Allah is the third of the three (in a Trinity)." But there is no Ilah (god) (none who has the right to be worshipped) but One Ilah (God-Allah). And if they cease not from what they say, verily, a painful torment will befall on the disbelievers among them (Surah 5:73).[4]

One difficulty that arises from the Qur'an's teachings about the Trinity is that Muslims have been led to greatly misunderstand what the Christian doctrine of the Trinity actually claims. What they are left with is, at best, a modalistic[5] view of the Trinity and a misrepresentation of the person of Jesus Christ.[6] What makes matters worse is that Muslim apologists have been exposed to faulty analogies that Christians themselves have used in their attempts to explain the Trinity.

Furthermore, the Qur'an reveals that Muhammad incorrectly assumed that Christians worship both Jesus and Mary as God, in addition to God Himself:

And (remember) when Allah will say (on the Day of Resurrection): "O 'Îsa (Jesus), son of Maryam (Mary)! Did you say unto men: 'Worship me and my mother as two gods besides Allah'?" He will say: "Glory be to You! It was not for me to say what I had no right (to say). Had I said such a thing, You would surely have known it. You know what is in my inner-self though I do not know what is in Yours; truly, You, only You, are the All-Knower of all that is hidden (and unseen)" (Surah 5:116).

The New Testament never represents the Godhead in this way. Nor does it ever say that worship should go to anyone other than God. There is agreement between the Bible and the Qur'an that worship should be directed only to God; but the major difference is that the Qur'an says that no one else should receive worship—not even Jesus.

> They (Jews and Christians) took their rabbis and their monks to be their lords besides Allah (by obeying them in things which they made lawful or unlawful according to their own desires without being ordered by Allah), and (they also took as their Lord) Messiah, son of Maryam (Mary), while they (Jews and Christians) were commanded [in the Taurat (Torah) and the Injeel (Gospel)] to worship none but One Ilah (God-Allah) La ilaha illa Huwa (none has the right to be worshipped but He). Praise and glory be to Him (far above is He) from having the partners they associate (with Him) (Surah 9:31).

The New Testament makes it clear that worship is to be given to God alone. When John began to worship an angel in Revelation 22:9, the angel said, "Do not do that. I [an angel] am a fellow servant of yours [John] and of your brethren the prophets and of those who heed the words of this book. Worship God." Yet the New Testament also records that Jesus received worship as God on numerous occasions.[7] Jesus did not reject this worship, which serves as an affirmation that He Himself was God.

In contrast to Islamic monotheism (Dynamic Monarchianism), Christianity presents monotheism in a triune Godhead. The Christian case for the Trinity is built on three biblical truths: (1) There is only one God[8]; (2) the Father, Son and Holy Spirit are called "God"[9]; (3) the Father, Son, and Holy Spirit are unique persons, not the same person.[10] This perspective is often denied by Islamic apologists like Shabir Ally[11] and the late Ahmed Deedat,[12] who consistently present the Father, Son, and Holy Spirit as three separate Gods and thus illogical. While it is true the Trinity teaches three separate personages, it is important to note that the distinction goes beyond the meaning of a person or persona. While the English word *person* is the best way to describe the separation of the entities within the Godhead, the term, when used in connection with the Trinity, may be better understood as "a subsistence in the divine essence— a subsistence which, while related to the other two, is distinguished from them by incommunicable properties."[13]

— QUESTIONS FOR DISCUSSION —

The Qur'an teaches that Jesus was just a messenger, a prophet, and certainly not deity. He is to be revered and obeyed, but not worshipped as God. By contrast, the Bible establishes that the one true God exists in a plurality that consists of three separate personages who are coequal, coeternal, and coexistent. Jesus is presented as and makes claims of His divinity in all four Gospels.

- What are the differences in how the Qur'an explains the Trinity, as compared to how the Bible explains the Godhead?

- If Jesus is just a messenger or prophet, and not deity as the Qur'an teaches, then what message did He come to deliver?

- What prophecies of Jesus are in the Qur'an, and do they agree with the prophecies of Jesus found in the Bible?

- In John's Gospel, Jesus received worship from Thomas. Would you like to see what Jesus's reaction was, according to John 20:28-29?

> Thomas answered and said to Him, "My Lord and my God!" Jesus said to him, "Because you have seen Me, have you believed? Blessed are they who did not see, and yet believed" (John 20:28-29).

Chapter 12

Jesus of the Qur'an Was Not Crucified on the Cross

*The Jesus of the Qur'an was a coward. He escaped, went to a cave,
and Allah raptured Him. Allah took Jesus like he took Elijah.*

ELIJAH, FORMER SHIA MUSLIM
(Interview—see chapter 18)

The Qur'an clearly states that Jesus was not crucified, but its details as to who really did die on the cross are ambiguous. And the uncertainty is heightened by the fact there is only one passage that mentions the crucifixion:

> And because of their saying (in boast), "We killed Messiah 'Îsa (Jesus), son of Maryam (Mary), the Messenger of Allah,"—but they killed him not, nor crucified him, but it appeared so to them [the resemblance of 'Îsa (Jesus) was put over another man (and they killed that man)], and those who differ therein are full of doubts. They have no (certain) knowledge, they follow nothing but conjecture. For surely; they killed him not [i.e. 'Îsa (Jesus), son of Maryam (Mary) عليهما السلام]:
>
> But Allah raised him ['Îsa (Jesus)] up (with his body and soul) unto Himself (and he عليه السلام is in the heavens). And Allah is Ever All-Powerful, All-Wise (Surah 4:157-158).

According to this passage, the Jews thought that they had killed Jesus, but they had not. Something happened that made them assume Jesus had died on the cross. Because the Qur'an is vague as to exactly what happened, various theories have developed in attempts to explain what the passage says.

Muslims from the Ahmadiyyab sect of Islam hold to an idea called the swoon theory. Ghulam Ahmad developed this theory in 1891. He moved away from the traditional Islamic understanding of the crucifixion by saying that Jesus had, in fact, been crucified. The theory states that Jesus was crucified, and that the Roman soldiers assumed He was dead when, in fact, He was not. He had merely swooned (or fainted), which is why, after He was placed in the tomb, He "rose again." "The 'burial spices' put on Jesus' body were actually medicines that helped revive him. Jesus appeared to his disciples, who mistook his recovery with a resurrection."[1]

While this theory is interesting, it is implausible given the severe scourging Jesus had received, His inability to carry the patibulum of His cross to the crucifixion site, the spikes driven through His wrists and feet, the fact He hung on the cross bleeding for six hours, and most notably that a spear pierced through His side and punctured His pericardial sac, releasing "blood and water."[2] These attested facts of crucifixion make it clear that Jesus suffered hypovolemic shock, which caused pericardial effusion; thus, among His causes of death would have been asphyxiation and congestive heart failure. Though scientific evidence substantially rules out the swoon theory, the greater obstacle for most Muslims is that no early sources support the Qur'an on this teaching.

The substitution theory is another attempt to explain Surah 4:157. This theory holds that one of Jesus's disciples was substituted for Him at the cross. There are a couple different variations to this theory. One says there was a mix-up at the crucifixion site, and one of Jesus's disciples was mistakenly crucified instead of Jesus. Another version states that Jesus asked someone to volunteer to be crucified for Him, and Simon of Cyrene accepted. Some even go as far as to say that it was Judas Iscariot who was crucified on the cross.[3] Others have contended that Allah allowed the similitude of Jesus to come upon one of the disciples so that some were deceived into believing that they had crucified Jesus.

This theory and its variants have a number of problems. First, if it were true, it would seem rather apparent that Jesus's mother and disciples would have been able to discern that it wasn't Jesus who had been nailed to the cross.[4] After all, they had witnessed the beating and scourging of Jesus. And the Romans, to put it lightly, were rather proficient at crucifying condemned individuals. The most problematic aspect of this theory is that it essentially accuses Allah of using trickery or deceit and causing many sincere followers to believe that Jesus had died.

If you were to accept the Qur'an's teaching that Jesus was not crucified, you would have to jettison the Gospels, which are eyewitness accounts of what had happened. Here a significant problem arises. The Gospels were written by eyewitnesses who wrote their accounts while many other eyewitnesses to the crucifixion were still alive. If Matthew, Mark, Luke, and John had been lying about what had happened, multitudes of people would have attested to the lie being perpetrated. Instead, you do not have to look far to see the various non-Christian historians who were willing to attest to not just the historicity of Jesus, but that He was crucified.

A number of first-century historians wrote about Jesus and His crucifixion. One such historian is Thallus, who corroborated the Gospel accounts of the earthquake and darkness that took place when Christ was crucified.[5] Tacitus, a Roman historian, wrote: "Christus, from whom the name had its origin, suffered the extreme penalty during the reign of Tiberius at the hands of one of our procurators, Pontius Pilatus..."[6] Mara Bar-Serapion, a Syrian philosopher, wrote about Jesus, whom he called the "wise King," saying, "What advantage did the Jews gain from executing their wise King? It was just after that that their kingdom was abolished."[7]

Phlegon, a Greek historian, wrote, "With regard to the eclipse in the time of Tiberius Caesar, in whose reign Jesus appears to have been crucified, and the great earthquakes which then took place..."[8] Roman historian Pliny the Younger, in a letter to the Roman emperor Trajan, wrote of the worship of Christ as God.[9] Other sources, such as Suetonius, Lucian of Samosata, Celsus, Emperor Trajan, and Emperor Hadrian all spoke of Christ. Even other later documents such as the Jewish Talmud, and the Toledot Yeshu spoke of Jesus and His life.

The most notable record comes from the Jewish historian Josephus (AD 37–101), who wrote,

> Now, there was about this time Jesus, a wise man, if it be lawful to call him a man, for he was a doer of wonderful works—a teacher of such men as receive the truth with pleasure. He drew over to him both many of the Jews, and many of the Gentiles. He was [the] Christ; and when Pilate, at the suggestion of the principal men amongst us, had condemned him to the cross, those that loved him at the first did not forsake him, for he appeared to them alive again the third day, as the divine prophets had fore-told these and ten thousand other wonderful things con-cerning him; and the tribe of Christians, so named from him, are not extinct at this day.[10]

Additional mentions of Jesus can be found in Josephus's writings, although there is some controversy regarding the passage cited above.[11]

The Qur'an's teaching that Jesus was not crucified has one other very significant obstacle to overcome—the early Christian hymn that Paul recounted in 1 Corinthians 15:3-5:

> I delivered to you as of first importance what I also received, that Christ died for our sins according to the Scriptures, and that He was buried, and that He was

raised on the third day according to the Scriptures, and
that He appeared to Cephas, then to the twelve.

The most noteworthy aspect of this early Christian hymn is its
date of origin. Paul said he had "received" this creed, which indicates it had already been circulating within the early church. How,
and when, did Paul receive this creed? If you date the crucifixion at
AD 33, then Paul's conversion would have occurred about three to
five years afterward (AD 36–38). Three years after his conversion,
he visited James and Peter in Jerusalem (AD 39–41). Therefore, one
could surmise that the creed was already in use within a few years of
the crucifixion. It's possible Paul could have received the creed when
he arrived in Damascus immediately after his conversion, "which
would make it even three years earlier, but the presence of the Sem-
itisms in the creed…in addition to the two proper names, favor
Jerusalem as the location where Paul first received it."[12] In addition
to mentioning the creed, Paul wrote of his interaction with eyewitnesses of the crucifixion and the resurrected Jesus in Galatians 1:18-
19 and 2:1-10.

QUESTIONS FOR DISCUSSION

According to the Qur'an, Jesus was not crucified, and thus never needed to be resurrected on the third day. Also, the identity of who died on the cross is uncertain. Though many Muslim scholars have attempted to give explanations such as the swoon theory and the substitution theory, a conclusive explanation seems out of reach. The Bible, on the other hand, is clear on what happened, and does not stand alone in what it says. Even non-Christian historians and government officials have explicitly and repeatedly confirmed that Jesus was indeed crucified on a cross.

- How does the Qur'an's teaching of the crucifixion differ from what first-century non-Christian historians have attested to?

- If Jesus was not crucified, what happened to Him? Why do Christians believe that He was, in fact, crucified?

- If Jesus was not crucified, why would Allah allow so many people to be deceived into thinking that He was?

- Paul repeated a creed that dates, at most, to a few years after the crucifixion. Would you like to consider what the first-century eyewitnesses had to say about what happened to Jesus according to 1 Corinthians 15:3-5?

  > ...Christ died for our sins according to the Scriptures, and that He was buried, and that He was raised on the third day according to the Scriptures, and that He appeared to Cephas, then to the twelve (1 Corinthians 15:3-5).

Chapter 13

Jesus of the Qur'an Did
Not Rise from the Dead

Jesus did not die. He will return to you on the Day of Resurrection.

IBN KATHĪR, FOURTEENTH-CENTURY MUSLIM SCHOLAR
(*Bulletin of the School of Oriental and African Studies*[1])

The Qur'an, as previously discussed, explicitly states that Jesus was not crucified. But if that is true, how did He die? The Qur'an is not clear on how or whether Jesus died, but it does attest that Allah raised Him up.

> And (remember) when Allah said: "O 'Īsa (Jesus)! I will take you and raise you to Myself and clear you [of the forged statement that 'Īsa (Jesus) is Allah's son] of those who disbelieve, and I will make those who follow you (Monotheists, who worship none but Allah) superior to those who disbelieve [in the Oneness of Allah, or disbelieve in some of His Messengers, e.g. Muhammad صلى الله عليه وسلم, 'Īsa (Jesus), Musa (Moses), etc., or in His Holy Books, e.g. the Taurat (Torah), the Injeel (Gospel), the Qur'an] till the Day of Resurrection. Then you will return to Me and I will judge between you in the matters in which you used to dispute" (Surah 3:55).

The Qur'an presents a much different understanding of the life of Jesus than the Bible. For example, Jesus's death was prophesied in the pages of the Old Testament and later fulfilled in the Gospels. Isaiah presents one of the more graphic prophetic writings concerning Jesus's death.

> He was pierced through for our transgressions, He was crushed for our iniquities; the chastening for our well-being fell upon Him, and by His scourging we are healed…He was oppressed and He was afflicted…By oppression and judgment He was taken away…For the transgression of my people, to whom the stroke was due?…But the LORD was pleased to crush Him, putting Him to grief; if He would render Himself as a guilt offering…He poured out Himself to death, and was numbered with the transgressors; yet He Himself bore the sin of many, and interceded for the transgressors (Isaiah 53:5,7-8,10,12).

In addition, Psalm 22 prophesied specific details about Jesus's sufferings:

> My God, my God, why have You forsaken me? Far from my deliverance are the words of my groaning…All who see me sneer at me; they separate with the lip, they wag the head, saying, "Commit yourself to the LORD; let Him deliver him; let Him rescue him, because He delights in him."…For dogs have surrounded me; a band of evildoers has encompassed me; they pierced my hands and my feet. I can count all my bones. They look, they stare at me; they divide my garments among them, and for my clothing they cast lots (Psalm 22:1,7-8,16-18).

The resurrection was of paramount importance to the early Christians. Jesus's crucifixion was necessary so that He could fulfill the prophecies laid out in Scripture. But without the resurrection, His crucifixion, miracles, and claims were worthless. Paul pointed to this all-important truth in 1 Corinthians 15. In the last chapter we looked at the creed cited in 1 Corinthians 15:3-5 and examined the attestation that Jesus died for our sins, was buried, and rose on the third day according to the Scriptures, and that there were post-resurrection appearances in which Jesus appeared before many witnesses. This creed was the cornerstone of belief for early Christians; it was and is the foundation for biblical Christianity and the gospel. Paul believed this and emphasized the centrality of the resurrection in the Christian faith. Consider his words to the Corinthians:

> If Christ has not been raised, then our preaching is vain, your faith also is vain. Moreover we are even found to be false witnesses of God, because we testified against God that He raised Christ, whom He did not raise, if in fact the dead are not raised. For if the dead are not raised, not even Christ has been raised; and if Christ has not been raised, your faith is worthless; you are still in your sins. Then those also who have fallen asleep in Christ have perished. If we have hoped in Christ in this life only, we are of all men most to be pitied (1 Corinthians 15:14-19).

It is clear that *if* the resurrection did not occur, then Christianity is a fraud and should be ignored, if not spoken against. Paul went on to say, "But now Christ has been raised from the dead, the first fruits of those who are asleep" (verse 20). He stated the resurrection of Jesus as fact, and that is not surprising because he himself was an eyewitness to the resurrected Jesus. Therefore, we can surmise that if Jesus was resurrected, then Christianity is true and should be accepted.

So, was Christ resurrected or not? Can we trust the eyewitness testimonies from the New Testament?

Dr. Gary Habermas, philosopher and Christian apologist, has compiled a number of "minimal facts" about the crucifixion and resurrection that are agreed upon by virtually all scholars—both secular and Christian. Among these facts are that Jesus died, was buried, and the tomb was empty a few days later. The disciples believed they literally saw the risen Jesus, which caused them to become transformed from doubters to bold proclaimers. The resurrection was central to their preaching and was proclaimed in Jerusalem, where Jesus had been crucified and buried. James, the brother of Jesus, who had originally been a skeptic, was converted to the faith. And Paul, who had been a persecutor of the church and put Christians to death, was converted after reportedly seeing the resurrected Jesus.[2] When you work through these widely accepted "minimal facts," the only likely conclusion is that the resurrection did indeed occur.

While there are a number of historical accounts that point to the likelihood of the resurrection, the question remains: What does the Qur'an say happened to Jesus? There are two additional passages that speak of the end of Jesus's time on Earth:

> Never did I say to them aught except what You (Allah) did command me to say: "Worship Allah, my Lord and your Lord." And I was a witness over them while I dwelt amongst them, but when You took me up, You were the Watcher over them; and You are a Witness to all things. (This is a great admonition and warning to the Christians of the whole world) (Surah 5:117).

> And Salam (peace) be upon me the day I was born, and the day I die, and the day I shall be raised alive! (Surah 19:33).

Surah 5:117, along with Surah 3:55, suggests that Allah raised Jesus up at some point. Some Muslim scholars suggest that this occurred at the crucifixion as part of the substitution theory.[3]

What is interesting is that Surah 19:33 quotes Jesus as saying that peace would be upon Him from the day He was born until the day of His death, and that He would be raised alive. One Muslim scholar, Mahmoud M. Ayoub, said,

> The Quran, as we have already argued, does not deny the death of Christ. Rather, it challenges human beings who in their folly have deluded themselves into believing that they would vanquish the divine Word, Jesus Christ the Messenger of God. The death of Jesus is asserted several times and in various contexts.[4]

The difficulty with Ayoub's interpretation is that if Jesus did die, then when, according to the Qur'an, did He die, and when was He raised? Ayoub's view is a very difficult position to hold when you consider what the Qur'an says within the context of each passage. The Qur'an does not answer these questions with the same precision that the Bible does. Examining the biblical text, you will find that there are a number of passages that predict the death and resurrection of Jesus, and they are all consistent with one another.[5]

───── QUESTIONS FOR DISCUSSION ─────

The Qur'an declares that Allah raised Jesus to heaven prior to the crucifixion, and that Jesus stated that He would die. Did Jesus die, or did He ascend to heaven? This is a difficult question to settle using the Qur'an. However, the Bible is clear in that it consistently states that Jesus was crucified, buried, and raised from the dead.

- Does the Qur'an teach that Jesus was raised up by Allah, as stated in Surah 3:55 and Surah 5:117? Or did He die, as stated in Surah 19:33?

- Given the "minimal facts" agreed upon by most scholars, is it reasonable to believe that the resurrection could have occurred?

- If Jesus did die, then when, according to the Qur'an, did He die, and when was He raised?

- Paul emphasized the importance of the resurrection to Christianity and the gospel message. How important do you think the resurrection is, based on what Paul wrote in 1 Corinthians 15:14-19?

> If there is no resurrection of the dead, not even Christ has been raised; and if Christ has not been raised, then our preaching is vain, your faith also is vain…But now Christ has been raised from the dead, the first fruits of those who are asleep (1 Corinthians 15:13-14,20).

Chapter 14

Jesus of the Qur'an Is
Not the Savior of the World

There's no concept of a savior in Islam.

ZIA HASSAN, FORMER MUSLIM
(Interview—see chapter 17)

Central to the veracity of Christianity are the teachings that Jesus is the Savior of the world who came to save His people from their sins by becoming the Lamb of God, giving His life as a sacrifice for their sins, and rising again from the grave. These are among the most prominent and consistent truths found throughout the New Testament. Here are just a few examples:

> She will bear a Son; and you shall call His name Jesus, for He will save His people from their sins (Matthew 1:21).

> If anyone wishes to come after Me, he must deny himself, and take up his cross and follow Me. For whoever wishes to save his life will lose it, but whoever loses his life for My sake and the gospel's will save it (Mark 8:33-34).

> Today in the city of David there has been born for you a Savior, who is Christ the Lord (Luke 2:11).

> We have heard for ourselves and know that this One is indeed the Savior of the world (John 4:42).

> After he brought them out, he said, "Sirs, what must I

do to be saved?" They said, "Believe in the Lord Jesus, and you will be saved, you and your household" (Acts 16:30-31).

Now I make known to you, brethren, the gospel which I preached to you…by which also you are saved…For I delivered to you as of first importance what I also received, that Christ died for our sins according to the Scriptures, and that He was buried, and that He was raised on the third day according to the Scriptures (1 Corinthians 15:1-4).

It is a trustworthy statement, deserving full acceptance, that Christ Jesus came into the world to save sinners, among whom I am foremost of all (1 Timothy 1:15).

By this the love of God was manifested in us, that God has sent His only begotten Son into the world so that we might live through Him. In this is love, not that we loved God, but that He loved us and sent His Son to be the propitiation for our sins (1 John 4:9-10).

They sang a new song, saying, "Worthy are You to take the book and to break its seals; for You were slain, and purchased for God with Your blood men from every tribe and tongue and people and nation" (Revelation 5:9).

Thus, it is rather surprising to find Muslim apologists claiming that the Bible—and more specifically, the New Testament—contradicts the claim that Jesus is the Savior. One Islamic website, Submission.org, declares:

We have been receiving many e-mails from our Christian brothers and sisters in which they preach to us that Jesus Christ is the Savior and the way. With due respect to them, we cannot accept their notion as it contradicts every known divine scripture including the Old Testament, the New Testament and the Final Testament (Quran).[1]

Whereas the Bible proclaims Jesus as the Savior of the world, the Qur'an makes no such claim. As we found earlier, the Qur'an denies that Jesus died on the cross and that He rose again. These acts are essential elements of the salvation message in the Christian gospel. It is because of Jesus's death and resurrection that He is able to save. Take away His cross and deny His resurrection, then Jesus is no longer the Savior.

The Qur'an clearly rejects the idea that the people of God "must believe in him" as Savior or as anything more than "a Messenger of Allah." To those believing Jesus to be anything more, the Qur'an warns that Jesus Himself "will be a witness against them" on the Day of Judgment.

> And there is none of the people of the Scripture (Jews and Christians) but must believe in him ['Îsa (Jesus), son of Maryam (Mary), as only a Messenger of Allah and a human being] before his ['Îsa (Jesus) عليه السلام) or a Jew's or a Christian's] death (at the time of the appearance of the angel of death). And on the Day of Resurrection, he ['Îsa (Jesus)] will be a witness against them (Surah 4:159).

SACRIFICE OF THE BELOVED SON IN THE QUR'AN

The concept of Jesus being a sacrificial Lamb of God, a sin offering, or a substitute is offensive to Islam. It is interesting, however, that the idea that God would demand the sacrifice of a beloved son is not foreign to the Qur'an. Both the Bible and Qur'an contain parallel accounts of Abraham being instructed by God to sacrifice his "only son." Despite important differences in the stories,[2] both sources describe Abraham symbolically offering his son as a sacrifice on an altar, at which point God "ransomed him with a great sacrifice."

Then, when they had both submitted themselves (to the Will of Allah), and he had laid him prostrate on his forehead (or on the side of his forehead for slaughtering); We called out to him: "O Abraham! You have fulfilled the dream!" Verily thus do We reward the Muhsinun (gooddoers—See 2:112). Verily, that indeed was a manifest trial. And We ransomed him with a great sacrifice (i.e. كبش - a ram) (Surah 37:103-107).

Christians consider the story from Genesis 22 to be a prophetic parallel to the gospel itself. Abraham was told to offer his "only son, whom you love"[3] and sacrifice him on the mountain of "the land of Moriah" (verse 2), in the very place that Jesus would later be crucified. When Abraham's son asked where the offering was, Abraham said, "God will provide for Himself the lamb" (verse 8).

The concept of atoning death, substitution, and sin sacrifice is not an obscure doctrine found solely in this account of Abraham's figurative sacrifice. It is a theme found throughout the Old Testament. It is seen in the sin covering for Adam and Eve (Genesis 3), the Passover lamb (Exodus 12), the sacrificial system of the tabernacle and temple (Leviticus 3), and Yom Kippur or the Day of Atonement (Leviticus 16). The Old Testament consistently affirms the ideas of ransom, sacrifice, and blood atonement. Indeed, "according to the Law, one may almost say, all things are cleansed with blood, and without the shedding of blood there is no forgiveness" (Hebrews 9:22).

IF JESUS IS NOT THE SAVIOR, WHO IS?

While the Qur'an clearly presents Allah as being merciful, in Islam there is nothing that corresponds to the Christian idea of someone dying for the sins of another. There is no promise of being freely forgiven through the vicarious sacrifice of someone else. The Bible, in contrast, offers this comforting assurance: "God demonstrates His own love toward us, in that while we were yet sinners, Christ died for us" (Romans 5:8). There is no such promise in the Qur'an.

Don Richardson, a Christian missiologist and the bestselling author of *Peace Child,* said that unlike the other cultures and religions he has studied, there were no redemptive analogies that can be made with Muslims. When it came to the core Christian concepts of substitution, sacrifice, sin offering, and propitiation, Islam offered no similar models or common ground to foster discussions. The Qur'an has so redefined the essentials of the Christian gospel as to make such an approach pointless.

> I approached the Qur'an after 9/11, and I began to study it intensively to see if the redemptive analogy approach could work for Christians to approach Muslims winsomely. But I found that everything that a Christian would use of redemptive analogy to lead a person to God was already redefined in the Qur'an by Muhammad in a way that made the redemptive analogy approach not work.[4]

In Islam there is no Christlike savior, and as a result, there is no assurance of salvation. For example, one Islamic website warns that being a Muslim does not mean one is promised salvation. For the Muslim, there is never a guarantee of avoiding hell:

> But let me continue just for a second. When we call to Islam, we do not promise you that if you're a Muslim you're saved, and we don't tell you that the best of the people we have are our teachers and leaders and they're going to the highest place.

> In fact, what we can guarantee you when you come to Islam is that a person can go to hell, there is no doubt about that. If you want to go to hell, that's easy, just be

disobedient to Allah, deny Him and that's where you will go. As far as our leaders and teachers, if they do not practice what they preach and if they preach one thing but live another, if they are, what we call "Munafiq" or hypocrites, they will be in the lowest part of hell, and Allah will start the fire of hell with them.[5]

QUESTIONS FOR DISCUSSION

There can be no assurance of salvation without a savior. Perhaps this is why even Muhammad seemed to have questions about his fate on the Day of Judgment, saying, "I know not what shall be done with me or with you" (Surah 46:9). Testimony from respected Hadith indicates that Muhammad was commenting on his eternal destiny.[6]

Christians, however, believe that they have a Savior who has paid the price for their sins and has purchased their salvation with His own blood (Acts 20:28). Thus, they have no doubts or fears about the Day of Judgment. They have assurance of salvation because of what the Savior has done for them. Not only do they have the promise of forgiven sins (Ephesians 1:7), they also have the goodness and righteousness of Jesus credited to their account (2 Corinthians 5:21).

- May I ask what a Muslim must do to avoid the fires of hell and live forever in paradise?

- Is it possible for you to have assurance that your sins have been forgiven?

- May I share with you a Christian scripture (1 John 5:11-13) that proclaims with certainty the assurance that comes with the gift of salvation?

> The testimony is this, that God has given us eternal life, and this life is in His Son. He who has the Son has the life; he who does not have the Son of God does not have the life. These things I have written to you who believe in the name of the Son of God, so that you may know that you have eternal life.

Part 3:

Discussing Jesus
with Muslims

In Part 1, we looked at the significance of Islam as well as the purported source, content, and basic teachings of the Qur'an. In Part 2, we learned what the Qur'an says and does not say about Jesus. We examined passages from the Qur'an and compared them to passages in the Bible to understand the issues that unite, and more significantly, divide the world's two largest religions. Here in Part 3, we will see how these issues play out in the lives of Muslims.

Chapter 15

The Debate: Jesus Christ— Prophet of Allah or Savior of the World?

*O*n October 29, 2017, a public debate was held between Islamic apologist Khalil Meek, executive director of the Muslim Legal Fund of America, and Christian apologist James Walker, president of Watchman Fellowship. The debate was hosted by the Bible & Beer Consortium (BBC), where Christians and atheists meet for formal debates held in clubs, local pubs, and other nonchurch settings. This was the first time the consortium sponsored a debate on Islam.

The debate topic was "Jesus Christ—Prophet of Allah or Savior of the World?" The debate moderator was Ezra Boggs, founder of BBC. The following is a transcript of the debate. This is the third such debate between Khalil and James, who, despite their differences, have been friends for more than ten years.

I hope this debate serves as a model for how friends can disagree yet discuss important issues respectfully, compassionately, and without compromise. I believe this debate will provide some helpful insight into the way Muslims interact with the subject matter of the previous chapters. Furthermore, I hope this debate will cause you to pray for my friend Khalil, as well as for any Muslims you may encounter in your sphere of influence.

Note: *The debate has a small number of minor edits made for the purpose of clarity.*

Ezra Boggs: Our online audience is screaming for you, Micah [the audio/video tech for Bible & Beer Consortium], I promise.

WHAT THE QUR'AN REALLY TEACHES ABOUT JESUS

Tonight's event the topic is "Jesus Christ—Prophet of Allah or Savior of the World?" Our first speaker is Khalil Meek. He's the executive director of the Muslim Legal Fund of America, which is the national charity leading the struggle against anti-Muslim injustice in American courtrooms. He converted to Islam around twenty years ago and has shared his journey to Islam with audiences across the world. He's also traveled to hundreds of communities to inform audiences about constitutional issues impacting Muslims in America.

As the organization's executive director, Meek spearheaded the initiatives to grant-fund Constitutional Law Center for Muslims in America, a nonprofit law firm dedicated to defending the legal rights of American Muslims. He also organized the Muslim Non-profit Leadership Conference, a series of conferences that delivers important information on legal and social challenges facing the Muslim community. Speaking to tonight's topic "Jesus Christ—Prophet of Allah or Savior of the World?" please welcome Khalil Meek [applause].

Khalil Meek: Thank you. Tonight, before I begin, by a show of hands, how many of you now on a scale of one to ten would rate yourself as a ten on Islam? One. Okay, a five or better? Two. Less than five? Above a one? How many ones? This presentation is geared toward the one. Tonight, I wanted to be able to share with anybody in the audience because I wasn't sure what the audience would be. [I want to share about] the Muslim perspective of Jesus, salvation in Islam (to use a Christian term), and make sure that the point of view and the reference of Jesus in Islam is made very clear.

Tonight, our debate will have to start with the reference point on your part. In other words, if you already had a background [in Islam], we could start arguing, but without a framework, you wouldn't understand the arguments. I have to build that framework in a short period of time. It's not hard, but you need it. We'll start tonight, and this will give you a framework for how a Muslim sees the world because we pray five times a day, seven days a week, 365 days out of the year.

If you've ever wondered what those prayers are, it's the exact same prayer every single time. Tonight, we'll start our program by me reading the prayer in English so you'll understand what a Muslim is doing when you see them in the airport or in a prayer line or in a mosque or anywhere you might witness a Muslim praying. This is what we're saying, the exact same thing over and over again.

> In the name of God most gracious most merciful, praise be the God, the cherisher, the sustainer of all the worlds, most gracious, most merciful, master of the Day of Judgment. You alone do we worship, you alone do we ask for help. Guide us to the straight path, the path on those that you've bestowed your grace and not the path of those who've earned your wrath, not the ones who've gone astray. Amen.

We'll start tonight by that prayer, which leads us to who is Jesus, and by form of reference, that would mean who is Mary in Islam. We'll start with Mary.

Mary in Islam is one of the most revered personalities [and] women who ever set foot on Earth. Muslims love and revere Mary as the mother of Jesus, peace be upon her. Mary is considered pious, chaste, pure, and virtuous. Mary is regarded as the best of women ever created. Muslims believe in the virgin birth of Jesus.

Mary is the only woman mentioned by name in the Qur'an. There is an entire chapter in the Qur'an named after Mary, Maryam. There is an entire chapter in the Qur'an named after Mary's father, Imran. What does the Qur'an have to say about Jesus, or who is Jesus to a Muslim? We'll start with the Qur'an speaking for itself.

First, I guess I'll explain what Muslims believe, then I'll get to the Qur'an, but Jesus is known as *'Īsa* in Arabic. Muslims love, respect, honor, and revere Jesus. Jesus is considered a great messenger prophet. Jesus was born from the virgin Mary. Jesus is a word from God; however, Muslims do not consider Jesus to be divine, and Muslims do not consider Jesus to be the Son, in any literal sense, of God.

There are titles of Jesus mentioned in the Qur'an. He's mentioned in over twenty-five places in the Qur'an, always with honor and respect. Jesus is mentioned as the son of Mary, the Messiah, the Christ, servant of God, messenger of God, the word of God, spirit from God, sign from God.

Now, we'll let the Qur'an speak. Behold the angel said,

> "Oh Mary, God has chosen you and purified you, chosen you above all women of all nations. Oh Mary, God gives you good news of a word from him whose name shall be Christ Jesus the Son of Mary, honored in this world and the hereafter and one of those nearest to God." Then Mary says, "Oh my lord, how shall I have a son when no man has touched me?" God said, "Even so God creates what he wills when God decrees a thing, He says to it be and it is. God will teach him—Jesus, the book and wisdom, the law and the gospel and appoint Jesus a messenger to the children of Israel" [Surah 3:42-49].

But the Qur'an says that, truly the likeness of Jesus with God is the likeness of Adam or as the likeness of Adam. He, God, created Adam from dust, and then said to Adam, "Be," and Adam was. The power of God is unlimited. God created Adam from dust—no man, no woman. God took a rib from Adam and created Eve, a man with no wife. God spoke to Mary and said, "Be," and Jesus was. God can create how God wishes, but being created separates you from the Creator.

Jesus being the Son of God, this is what the Qur'an specifically says about this relationship:

> They say, "God has taken unto himself a son, glory be to God. Nay to God belongs all that is in the heaven and

earth, all are subservient to him. The originator of the heavens and earth, when Allah decrees a thing he says to it be and it is" [al-Baqarah 2:116].

In the Qur'an it says,

"Say he is Allah or God the one and only, God the eternal, the absolute, God begets not nor was he begotten, and there's nothing comparable to Him. They do blaspheme who say God is one of three in a trinity, for there is no God except the one God." Christ, the son of Mary, was no more than a messenger. Many were the messengers who passed away before him, "Oh, people of the book" [Surah 5:73].

That's a reference the Qur'an uses repeatedly for Christians and Jews:

Oh, people of the book, commit no excess in your religion, nor say of God anything but the truth [Surah 4:171].

Jesus, or Christ Jesus the son of Mary, was no more than a messenger of God. A word which He bestowed on Mary, a spirit preceding from Him. Believe in God and His messengers, say not Trinity— desist, it will be better for you. For God is one God, glory be to Him. Far exalted is God above having a son. To God belongs all things in heaven and on Earth, and enough is God as a disposer of affairs.

Behold God would say, "Oh, Jesus, son of Mary, did you say to men worship me and my mother as God?" A degradation of God and Jesus will say, "Glory be to thee, never could I say what I had no right to say. Had I said such a thing, you would indeed have known it. You know what is in my heart, though I know not what is in yours, for you know what's in for all that is hidden" [Qur'an 5:116]. Such was Jesus, the son of Mary. It is a statement of truth about which they vainly dispute.

It is not befitting for the majesty of God that He should beget a son, glory be to Him. When God determines a matter, He says to it, "Be," and it is. Verily, God is my Lord and your Lord; therefore, serve ye, that is the way that is straight. Say, "Oh, people of the book, exceed not in your religion the bounds of what is proper, trespassing beyond the truth, nor follow the vain desires of people who went wrong in times gone by, who misled and strayed (themselves) from the even way" or the truth [Surah 5:77].

That's what the Qur'an has to say about this topic. For that to have more reference, I'd like to quickly introduce you to the theology of Islam. To do that, you need a brief introduction to a little bit about Islam and Muslims. It's one religion with many cultures; there are fifty-seven countries in the world that have a majority population of Muslims. Out of the fifty-seven, there are twenty-two that are Arab countries—roughly 1.6 billion Muslims in the world today, roughly a fourth of the population.

Of all of those Muslims, only one-fifth of those Muslims are Arab, so four out of five Muslims are not Arab, and the country with the largest Muslim population is Indonesia. Islam is a monotheistic religion, inviting all people to recognize, believe, and worship God; believe in heaven and hell; believe in the Day of Judgment; do what's right, forbid what's wrong; and follow divine guidance. Islam is a universal message and religion. Islam is a comprehensive way of life for anyone, anytime, and anywhere in the world.

Islam is a faith of human unity; it calls all mankind regardless of race or gender to unite in the worship of the one true God. Islam considers all people as brothers and sisters, rejects discrimination on the basis of gender, color, race, or ethnic background. Mankind is one family. There is an illustration [pointing to his PowerPoint presentation]. Here's another. This is the Kaaba in Mecca. If you've never been there, that little black box in the center is what's referred to as the Kaaba. There's a stadium built around it now.

Those are people performing the ritual of hajj once a year—men, women, children, rich, poor, from every country on earth, standing side by side and worshipping the same. These are just more pictures to give you an idea. Two to three million people a year perform that pilgrimage. What is Islam? The word itself is an Arabic word that comes from the root word *peace*, but it contains in the meaning "salam," [which] means "willful surrender, peaceful submission, voluntary obedience."

Muslims believe everyone has a free will. With that free will, you're free to do as you please. If it feels good, do it, or if you choose, then you can obey divine guidance—what God has created you for and follow His commandments. Islam means to peacefully, willfully, and knowingly submit your personal free will to voluntarily accept and obey divine guidance. When you do that, it also contains the meaning that you will attain peace through that submission, so attaining mental, spiritual, and physical peace—peace with yourself, your creator, and others.

Islam is a verb; it's an action. If you learn Arabic, to show the one doing some action, they put a prefix before the verb, *mu*. In English, if you run, we add *er*, so you're a runner, swim/swimmer, jog/jogger, to show the one doing the action. In Arabic, a prefix of *mu* before a verb is the one doing the verb, so *mu-Islam* is a Muslim—someone practicing the act of Islam, willful submission to divine guidance. Muslims follow the creator and this divine guidance; [they follow] who is the creator and what is the guidance.

The Muslims call the creator God Allah. Some people call Him Yahweh, Adonai, Elohim, Jehovah. In the Semitic language—Allah, Illah, all the same—they mean exactly the same thing: Allah. In Hebrew, hallelujah, it's exactly the same meaning, so praise God, praise be to the creator. If you would take an English Bible and translate it into Arabic, to convert them to Christianity, this is one example in Genesis—the first eight verses, you'd find the word *Allah* ten times in the first eight verses of Genesis to the Arabic-speaking audience so that you would communicate with them.

It's not a foreign God, it's not a strange God, it is the word for God in Arabic. The God, the creator, the unique, the one and only, the cherisher, the sustainer, the sovereign, the almighty, the real, the eternal, *Allah* is the proper name for God in Arabic. It also does not contain gender. Allah has no gender, Allah is not masculine or feminine, Allah has no mother or father, Allah has no children or relatives, Allah is not part of the creation, Allah is the creator.

In fact, if you or I can touch it, taste it, see it, smell it, it is not Allah. If it's tangible, part of the universe, it is not part of what Allah is. Allah is the creator and the sovereign, and he wills the creation into being. "There is no God but Allah" is a concept called *tawhid*, and tawhid means pure monotheism, the complete oneness in reference to God. God has no equals, no partners, nothing worthy of worship except Allah.

Nothing [is] worthy of praise but Allah; Allah has power over all things. Everything is dependent upon Allah. Allah is not dependent on anything. Allah is perfect, supreme, sovereign. Allah deserves all reverence, worship, praise, respect, and devotion. Again, if you can touch it, taste it, see it, smell it, it is not Allah.

In the Qur'an:

> Allah, there's no God but He, the Living, the Self-subsistent, Eternal. No slumber can seize him or sleep. His are all things in the heaven and on earth. Who is there who can intercede in His presence except as He permits? He knows what's before you, what's after them and they comprehend nothing of His knowledge except what He wills. His Throne comprises the heavens and earth, and preserving them the Most High, the Supreme (in glory) [Surah 2:255].

In the Qur'an, Allah refers to Himself in ninety-nine different names; each attribute is descriptive of a perfect or supreme quality and precludes any kind of defect or weakness. Each attribute is expressed in a way that can be understood by an average person. Each attribute confirms the idea of tawhid, the oneness of God, meaning God is the only essence of that attribute.

Each attribute belongs only to Allah. For example, these are the ninety-nine names of Allah. I won't read them, but I'll leave them there for a second for anybody to scan through them—the most compassionate, the merciful, the shaper, the creator, the majestic, the forgiving, the appreciative, the loving one, the truth, the ultimate, protector, the first and the last. I doubt James would argue with any of these attributes, but he's free to do so.

These attributes give us a very clear understanding of what God is, but not in a tangible physical sense. This is monotheism, [it is] expressed very clearly in the Qur'an. We read it before, "Say, 'He is Allah, the one and only, the eternal, the absolute he begets not nor is he begotten and there is nothing comparable to him.'" Now, when it comes to monotheism, Islam is considered or considers itself a sister religion to the monotheistic Abrahamic faiths.

When the Muslim says, "We believe in one God and all that has been sent down, then what was sent down to Abraham, Ishmael, Isaac, Jacob, and the prophets, the tribes of Israel, and that which was given to Moses and to Jesus and all that was given to the other prophets from their Lord," we do not differentiate in faith between any of them. Thus we are Muslims in willing submission to Allah or to God alone. We believe all those prophets were Muslim.

We believe Abraham was a Muslim, Moses was a Muslim, Jesus was a Muslim—because, by definition, they submitted their free will to divine guidance as prophets. They led their people to the oneness of God, so by definition, they would be Muslim. When we say, "We believe in the Torah, the Psalms, the Gospel, and the Qur'an," we make no distinction between any of them. We believe that if Moses were here today, every word out of his mouth we would accept as true.

Jesus, every word out of His mouth we accept as true. Every

word out of Muhammad's mouth, of the Qur'an, is true... [T]his is a verse in the Qur'an [paraphrasing Surah 5:48], now "we have sent down to you O Muhammad the scripture, the Qur'an, in truth as a confirmation of all the Scripture that preceded it and a guardian over it, preserving it."

We believe in the Torah, in the Psalms, in the proverbs, in the Gospel of the Injil, the good news of Jesus, and in the Qur'an. This is just a partial list of the prophets, but we've already mentioned several of them—David, Solomon, Ezekiel, Daniel, Hosea, Joel, Amos.

The character of a Muslim and a Christian or someone of a monotheistic face would be identical. These are the personal moral ethics of a Muslim, which should not differ from a Christian; every page of the Qur'an speaks to one of these ethics. Faith requires action, do good, forbid wrong, be educated, seek knowledge, have integrity, be honest, sincere, modest, humble, pious. Be pure, clean and sober, just, noble, steadfast, show forgiveness, be kind and generous, be optimistic, thankful, and happy. Obey the commandments of God, trust God with all your heart, soul, and mind.

These are personal moral ethics. You can randomly open the Qur'an, on any page you will find them. The same is also true of societal moral ethics—how we should behave as a group. Mankind is one family; if one person suffers, everyone suffers. All life is sacred, all human rights should be protected, love one another, show moderation in everything. Love for others what you love for yourself; take care of the orphans, the widows, the needy; defend the weak; free the oppressed; fill your trust, commitments, and promises; be just. Again, I don't see any exception between the two, but for clarity, because most people know nothing about Islam, this is what a Muslim sees when they look in the mirror—when a Muslim says we believe in God, we believe in Allah, we believe in the Creator, we believe in the prophets.

How do we go to heaven? What is salvation for a Muslim? Salvation for a Muslim is as simple as the concept of pure monotheism.

As a Muslim, if you believe there is no God but the creator, and you associate nothing with that creator, have pure monotheism, and that understanding of tawhid that is salvation for a Muslim, you will go to heaven. If you associate anything that you can touch, taste, see, feel—any tangible thing, be it a person, a cow, a star, a tree, a rock, anything—you will go to hell. The salvation lies in your belief of one God and associating nothing with that God.

Islam is a complete way of life. You start with that conclusion: I believe there is a creator, I believe that creator is one, and I want to follow that guidance. There's an entire way of life to support that conclusion. But if you don't have that conclusion to start with, you can pray, fast, give zakat, go to hajj, do all of the rituals, and [still] go straight to hell. None of that will do you any good; all that is a support mechanism to stay on God, [stay] conscious on that conclusion. Your salvation lies in tawhid, the oneness of your Creator.

For Jesus to be a prophet of Islam would be the only way a Muslim could even see Jesus, and we are taught He is one of the mightiest messengers of God, the prophet of God. Everything about Jesus we accept. When it comes to a Trinity—God the Father, the Son, the Holy Ghost, He died for our sins—this is where a Muslim and a Christian would separate and have an ocean of difference in salvation. We would have the same of everything before then that we could agree on. Doesn't mean we're any closer than [when] we started, but if there's a difference between a Christian and a Muslim, this is it.

It lies in how we perceive our relationship with God and how we define salvation and what it takes to get to heaven.

How much time have I used? I don't even know when I started. Anyway, I'm done with that, so thank you, and I will let James come and explain his…

Ezra: Khalil Meek [applause]. Our second presenter is James Walker, president of the Watchman Fellowship. [He is a] former fourth-generation Mormon with over twenty-five years of ministry experience in the fields of Christian countercult, evangelism, apologetics, and discernment. He interviewed as an expert on new religious movements and cults on a variety of network television programs, including *Nightline, ABC World News Tonight,* and *The NewsHour* with Jim Lehrer. He's spoken at hundreds of churches, colleges, universities, and seminaries throughout the United States and internationally.

Reverend Walker joined the staff of Watchman in 1984, became the president in 1994. Watchman Fellowship is a nonprofit educational organization headquartered in Arlington, Texas. Watchman Fellowship is an apologetics and discernment ministry that provides research and evaluation on cults, the occult, and new religious movements from a traditional Christian perspective. Because of his own background and his love for those in new religious movements and alternative faiths, James Walker has invested his life into reaching them with the true gospel of Jesus Christ.

His desire is to work together with local churches, train and equip believers to reach out to those of other faiths by earnestly contending for the faith [Jude 3], for speaking the truth in love [Ephesians 4:15]. Please welcome, speaking of the topic "Jesus Christ—Prophet of Allah or Savior of the World?" James Walker [applause].

James Walker: First of all, I want to say thank you to Ezra, to Micah, to the Bible and Beer Consortium for envisioning and sponsoring this event—appreciate that. Also for the Door Club, for providing the venue, and most of all, for my friend Khalil Meek, for being willing to take time out of his busy schedule to come and present the Muslim understanding of this important issue: Who is Jesus? Now, we are using a debate format tonight, but I think I would not be putting words in Khalil's mouth that this is not about winning an argument or defeating an opponent.

It really is about a better understanding for both of us, for all of us here, to be able to understand the similarities, but more importantly, the differences between the world's two largest religions. While it's a debate in format, I think you'll find it to be much more friendly than anything that we saw last year in the presidential debates. I have the privilege tonight of presenting the Christian understanding of Jesus Christ, that He is the Savior of the world. I'm going to make the case this evening that Jesus Christ was a prophet, but more than that, He came to Earth for the express purpose of saving His people from their sins—that He died on the cross as a substitute; that His death, burial, and resurrection from the grave [were to give us] salvation, to forgive us of our sins, and for us to enjoy the presence of God for eternity. We do that by having our faith in Jesus Christ, by grace through faith alone, and that goes for all who put their faith and trust in Him.

Now, I think it will be best perhaps for me to start on common ground, and there are things we agree on—we are monotheistic religions. I have been to many of the debates here, it always seems to be a Christian and atheist, but this time it is two people [who] both believe in God; this is a first for the group here, but we do have things in common.

We believe in God, we believe in the supernatural, we believe in heaven, hell, we believe in the Day of Judgment—that much we have in common. The first part of tonight's question— Jesus Christ, was He a prophet?—on this we can completely agree. Let's start with the things that we do have in common. I want to address that issue— Jesus Christ, is He a prophet of God?...

Okay, let's start, if we could, with the things that we have in common—so we agree Jesus is a prophet of God. Again, this is something we do have in common with our Muslim neighbors, our Muslim friends—we believe that Jesus is definitely a prophet of God. This raises, I think, some very important questions, then. What did Jesus prophesy? If He is the prophet of God, the natural question I would have is to ask, What did Jesus prophesy? I would want to know the [answer to the] question, Were the prophecies of Jesus fulfilled? That's something [that] would be a natural thing to ask of myself and want to explore.

The third thing I want to know is, Did Jesus fulfill the prophecies of Isaiah 53, as well as the other prophecies in the Old Testament? Khalil just gave us a list of the number of the prophets in history, the world according to Islam, many of them being the biblical prophets. We talked about Isaiah and Ezekiel and King David, and even Adam, I think, would go in that category for the Muslim. Then the fourth question, the important one for the issue tonight: Can Jesus save His people by paying for their sins?

Now, [it's] interesting we raise these questions—that in the Qur'an, we find instructions given to Muhammad of when you are in doubt, where to go to get the answers to these kinds of questions. We find in the Qur'an a statement—this is Surah 10:94, "If you are in doubt Muhammad about that which we have revealed to you then ask those people of the book." Who would [we] ask? As Khalil already shared with us in his introduction, the people of the book would be the Jews and the Christians, as he goes on to say, who have been reading the Scriptures before you.

The Scriptures before them being the Torah, the Old Testament, the prophets, and the Gospel, the Injil, as Khalil shared with us. We are to go there, according to the Qur'an, to the Scriptures before you. "The truth has certainly come to you from your Lord so never be among the doubters," Surah 10:94—this is where we are to go. I know that when I have had these discussions with other Muslims, and probably Khalil would agree with them as well, that the difficulty of going to the people of the book today or going to the Scriptures today, or the New Testament, the earlier prophecies, the earlier Scriptures, is that they have been corrupted. The question arises, When were the Scriptures corrupted? That's an extremely important issue, because the answer to that question puts us somewhat on the horns of a dilemma.

When were the earlier Scriptures corrupted? You could say, "Well, it was before Muhammad." If it was before Muhammad, though, why would Allah send him to the corrupted book and the very people who corrupted it? Why would he tell them, "If you have questions or doubts, go to the people of the book, go to the Christians, and go to the Jews?"

Well, perhaps the Scriptures were corrupted after the time of Muhammad, but the evidence has already eliminated that possibility. We have manuscripts, codices, we have documents of both the Old and New Testaments dating far back before the time of Muhammad. We have the Scriptures that were in circulation at that time, and they agree with what we have today as Scripture.

That raises the issue, Was God unable or unwilling to preserve His original Scriptures? That to me is problematic, troubling, because if it were either one—it really doesn't matter whether He was unwilling to preserve or for some reason unable to preserve—then how can we know any truth, and for that matter, how can a Muslim have confidence that God would preserve the Qur'an when He was unable or unwilling to preserve the others?

I want to address the question, What [did] Jesus prophesy? [That's] my first question to come up, and I would like to go to that.

Jesus, first of all, prophesied that the Torah would not be corrupted, this is [in] Matthew chapter 5:18. [First], "It is easier for heaven and earth to pass away than for one dot of the law to become void"—that's Luke 16:17, and also verse 18. Matthew 5: "Truly I say to you, until heaven and earth pass away, not an iota nor a dot will pass from the law until all is accomplished."

What did Jesus prophesy, if He's a true prophet? He prophesied that the Torah would not be corrupted, that it would not pass away, that not one stroke, not one part of a letter, would pass away.

He also prophesied that about His own words. Jesus prophesied in Matthew 24:35, "Heaven and earth will pass away, but My words will not pass away." We have a prophecy by someone whom both religions look to and honor as a prophet, who is prophesying that His Word will not pass away, nor will the earlier scriptures found in the Old Testament.

Then I want to ask the question, What did Jesus prophesy? First of all, He prophesied His crucifixion, His death, and His resurrection in three days. Now, this is significant because this is denied in the Qur'an.

The Qur'an holds that the Jesus that they *thought* they had crucified, indeed they crucified Him not, and that there was no death, there was no resurrection three days later. But this is the heart of the Christian gospel. In Matthew chapter 20, beginning in verse 17, as Jesus is going up to Jerusalem, He took the twelve disciples aside and on the way, He said to them, "See that we are going up to Jerusalem, and the Son of Man"—here's the prophecy—"will be delivered over to the chief priests and scribes and they will condemn him to death and deliver him over to the Gentiles to be mocked, flogged, scourged, and crucified, and He will be raised on the third day."

If Jesus was a prophet of God, what did He prophesy? His death, burial, and resurrection. He also prophesied that Satan would tempt us to deny His death and His resurrection. In Matthew chapter 16 verse 21, we find this: "From that time Jesus began to show His disciples that He must go to Jerusalem and suffer for many things from the elders and the chief priests and scribes and be killed on the third day and on the third day be raised." Verse 22, "And Peter took Him aside and began to rebuke Him saying, 'Far be it from you, Lord, this shall never happen to You.' But He turned and said to Peter, 'Get behind me, Satan. You are a hindrance to Me, for you are not setting your mind on the things of God but on the things of man.'" Matthew chapter 16. So, what did Jesus prophesy?

In addition to that, He prophesied that the church who confesses that Jesus is the Son of God would never be overpowered by Satan. In Matthew 16, we find back in verse 13, "Now, when Jesus came into the district of Caesarea Philippi, He asked His disciples,

'Who do people say that the Son of man is?' And they said, 'Some say John the Baptist, and others Elijah, and others Jeremiah or one of the prophets.'" Now—this is, I think, significant, because this is exactly what Islam tells us.

This is what Muslims tell us—that Jesus was one of the prophets, one of the warners, one of many, but nothing more. We find Jesus's reply—He said to them, "But who do you say that I am?" Simon Peter replied, "You are the Christ, the Son of the living God." Now, as Khalil just eloquently explained to us, this is something that goes against the grain, it goes against tawhid, the idea of the oneness [of God].

In fact, it could be looked at as tantamount to a shirk, which is [a] virtually unpardonable sin. This is the one thing that, if you associate the attributes of deity of Allah God with anyone else, then this is the one thing that I think, [as] Khalil put it, will send you straight to hell—I think those were his words. Jesus certainly would have rebuked Peter for calling Him the Son of God, but what did He say? He goes on to say this: …"Blessed are you, Simon Bar-Jonah, for flesh and blood has not revealed this to you, but My Father, who is in heaven. And I tell you that you are Peter, and on this rock I will build My church, and the gates of hell shall not prevail against it."

Another thing—what [else did] Jesus prophesy? That He would raise Himself from the dead as a sign of His authority. In John chapter 2 we find, "The Jews said to Him, 'What sign do You show us for these things?' Jesus answer to them, 'Destroy this temple, and in three days I will raise it up.'"

Verse 20, then the Jews said, "It has taken forty-six years to build this temple." This is talking about Herod, the second temple, the remodeling that was being done more than forty-six years. Verse 21, "But He was speaking about the temple of His body. When therefore He was raised from the dead, His disciples remembered that He had said this." He prophesied—this is one of His prophecies.

[That's] the scriptures, that's the Torah, Word that Jesus had spoken; that's His prophecies.

Again, what did Jesus prophesy? He also prophesied [that] His crucifixion would result in glorification. This was not a mistake; this was not a terrible accident. This was ordained from the foundation—that Jesus would be the very Lamb of God who would die for and on behalf of His people, and be raised from the dead in order to give them eternal life. We found the prophecy of Jesus in John chapter 2:32: "And when I am lifted up from the earth, I will draw all men to myself." Verse 33: "And He said this to show what kind of death He was going to die, that He would be lifted up on the cross."

He also prophesied the purpose of His death, [which] was to pay a ransom to redeem His people from their sins. This is Mark 10:45: "For even the Son of Man came not to be served, but to serve, and to give His life a ransom for many."

Now, the second question I wanted to address this evening is—Jesus being a prophet of God—Were the prophecies of Jesus fulfilled? In other words, was He a true prophet? Did His prophecies actually come true? We can answer in the affirmative. This is 1 Corinthians chapter 15, beginning in verse 1—the apostle Paul is verifying the prophecies of Jesus: "Now, I would remind you, brothers, of the gospel preached to you, which you received, in which you stand and by which you are saved if you hold fast to the word I preach to you, unless you have believed in vain. For I delivered to you of first importance what I also received, that Christ died for our sins in accordance with the Scriptures."

The Scriptures talk about that time—I'd like to share with you from Isaiah and other Old Testament passages from the Psalms. [First Corinthians 15] verse four: "That He was buried, that He was raised on the third day in accordance with the Scriptures, and that He appeared to Cephas Peter, and then twelve, then he appeared to more than five hundred brothers at one time, most of whom are still alive, though some have fallen asleep."

What you have is—and this [is] significant—let me just say it's an aside: Other Muslim scholars or Muslims I've talked to—Muslim apologist Shabir Ally, for example—will complain that the Gospels were written very late. I do believe the Gospels had a rich oral tradition, just like the Qur'an, which was recited, was repeated orally before it was ever written down. But it is about a couple of decades perhaps after the events of the crucifixion. It was a different world than we live in, a constant day of twenty-four-hour news cycles and Twitter, Instagram, and Snapchat—things like that. You need to know this is much earlier.

First Corinthians 15 is within six years of the event. He's describing something that happened within six years of the event, the crucifixion, where the apostle Paul, after he came face to face with the risen Christ, met with the half brother of Jesus, James, in Jerusalem, as well as Jesus's closest disciple, Peter or Cephas, and verified the things that he's talking about. We have something very, very early, going back to just less than a decade after the events of the crucifixion and resurrection. Verse 7: "Then he appeared to James, and then all the apostles, last of all, as to one untimely born, He also appeared to me"—and Paul's referring to himself.

Did Jesus fulfill Isaiah 53? As Khalil shared with us, they believe not just in the prophet Muhammad, they believe Jesus was a prophet, and all the Old Testament prophets, including Isaiah. What did Isaiah prophesy? What's interesting [is] to see what the Qur'an says, which Khalil already shared with us about: "And We sent, following in their footseps, Jesus, the son of Mary, confirming that which came before him in the Torah; and We gave him the Gospel [the Injil], in which was guidance and light and confirming that which preceded it of the Torah as guidance and instruction for the righteous" [Surah 5:46].

Again, [what] the Qur'an says, Khalil also verified for us, looking back to the earlier prophets: What did they prophesy? Let's look at Isaiah...but let me first read to you from Matthew chapter 5:

"Don't think that I've come to abolish the Torah or the prophets," Jesus said. "I have come not to abolish, but to complete. Yes, indeed, I tell you that until heaven and earth pass away, not so much as a yod or a stroke will pass from the Torah—not until everything that must happen has happened."

Now, I chose Isaiah 53 in part because of the Great Isaiah Scroll. [It] is part of the Dead Sea scrolls, and this is a scroll—an intact scroll—of Isaiah. I got the chance to see this in Jerusalem; it dates back to about one hundred years before the time of Christ. This was the copy of Isaiah, this was the Isaiah that was contemporary with the Isaiah that Jesus quoted at the synagogue, and it was [what] the Ethiopian eunuch was reading on his way to Gaza from Jerusalem. We have this intact scroll which matches [and is] virtually identical to the Masoretic text, which is the foundation for our English Bibles today. Let me read to you, as much as I can get through, some of the remarkable prophecies of Isaiah about the coming of Jesus.

Isaiah 53:3: "And He was despised and rejected by men, a man of sorrows and acquainted with grief, and like one from whom men hide their faces, He was despised and we esteemed Him not. Surely, He has borne our griefs and carried our sorrows, yet we esteemed Him stricken and smitten as beaten by God and afflicted, but He was pierced for our transgressions." [Here we see] this idea that a substitutionary atonement can take the sins of someone else. "He was crushed for our iniquities. Upon Him was chastisement that brought us peace, and with His wounds we are healed."

"All we like sheep have gone astray, we've all turned everyone to his own way, and the Lord has laid on Him [this is on this suffering servant] the iniquity of us all." Verse 7: "He was oppressed, He was afflicted, yet He did not open His mouth. Like a lamb that was led to the slaughter, like a sheep that was before shearers, He opened not His mouth. By oppression in judgment He was taken away, and for us and for His generation, who considered that He was cut off out of the land of the living, stricken for the transgression of My people."

Verse 9: "And they made His grave with the wicked and with a rich man in His death, although He had done no violence, and there was no deceit in His mouth. Yet it was the will of the Lord to crush Him. He has put Him to grief when His soul makes an offering for guilt, He shall see His offspring, and shall not prolong His days; the will of the Lord shall prosper in His hand. As a result of the anguish of His soul, He will see it and be satisfied; by His knowledge shall the Righteous One, My Servant, will justify the many, as He shall bear their iniquities."

Again, this idea is foreign to Islam, but in the Old Testament, the New Testament, this is the idea of someone bearing the sins of someone else and making them right with God through substitution. Verse 12: "Therefore, I would divide Him the portion with the many. He shall divide the spoils with the strong, because He poured out His soul to death, and was numbered with the transgressors; yet He bore the sin of many, and makes intercession for the transgressors."

Did Jesus fulfill Isaiah 53? In Acts chapter 8, Luke, who wrote the Gospel of Luke and wrote the book of Acts, reports that Philip was led by an angel to meet an Ethiopian eunuch on the road from Jerusalem to Gaza. Philip found him reading the same passage, Isaiah 53, from the scroll of Isaiah. In verse 34, we pick up in Acts 8, "And the eunuch said to Philip, 'About whom I ask you, does the prophet say this? About himself or someone else?'"

He's talking about Isaiah 53, what we just read. Is this about Isaiah? Is he talking about himself, or someone else? Verse 35: "Then Philip opened his mouth and began with this scripture and told him the good news about Jesus." Jesus not only was a prophet whose prophecies were fulfilled, He also was the subject of fulfilled prophecies.

From Genesis chapter 3—from the promise that there would be one who would crush the head of the serpent—all the way through the Old Testament, we find fulfilled prophecies that pointed to Christ. I [want to] ask the most important question: Can Jesus save

His people by paying for their sins? The second half of our [topic] question for tonight asks, Is He the Savior of the world? In Islam, we [Christians] have an agreement—[both] monotheistic religions believe in the Day of Judgment, and Khalil and I would totally agree that we will stand before God one day.

In Islam, the idea is that there will be a great scale of justice. On one side, there are all your good deeds; on the other side, all your bad deeds. And your good deeds must outweigh your bad deeds.

Is my time up? Okay how much time do I have? Okay.

Let me read what the Qur'an says about the Day of Judgment, and this is from Surah 29:12: "And those who do disbelieve say to those who believe, 'Follow our way, and we will carry your sins, but they will not carry anything of their sins; indeed, they are liars.'" The Qur'an has the idea that someone can promise you that they will pay for your sins, but they have no ability to do that. They are lying when they do that.

However, interestingly, the very next verse does hint at something else: "But they will surely carry away their own burdens"— their own sins, in other words, and look at this—and "other burdens along with their burdens. Other sins besides sins that they committed they will be carrying. They surely will be questioned on the day of resurrection about what they used to invent" (Surah 29:13).

A very popular Muslim website has talked about this—www .myreligionislam.com. It says—Hadith Sharif says—"There is no human without sins." I think that we would agree with our Muslim friends. "For instance, if one breaks another's heart, the aggrieved party will have a right on the wrongdoer. Absolution from this right requires the wrongdoer to get the aggrieved party's forgiveness by offering an apology."

What will happen if the wronged party does not waive his or her rights? It's an interesting answer—what happens then? "It will be executed in the world to come by way of bartering"—listen to this—"bartering the wrongdoer's obligatory acts of worship for the harm given"—or this is the other alternative—"or the sins of the aggrieved party will be transferred to the wrongdoer." People's sins and rewards will be weighed on the [scales] and they will be treated according [to how they] weigh.

Now again the idea is this: Before you go to the Day of Judgment for your good deeds and your bad deeds to be weighed on the balance—you have to make things right with anyone you did wrong [against]. There will be a line of people to talk to you, and Islam says that they will one by one come to you, and if you did someone wrong, and they've not forgiven you, you have to barter with them and give some of your good deeds or your obligatory worship and give to them [so you can] offset the bad you did. But if you run out of good deeds, that's okay. You can take some of their sins, some of their bad deeds, into your account. [Some say,] "I don't think it's really that fair, in Islam, that someone can receive the benefit of someone else's good works, good works they never did."

On the other hand, one can also be punished for sins that they never committed. The idea of this substitution is built into the judgment day of Islam—of somebody else's sins being put in your account, or the reverse of that being true as well. In Islam, my bad deeds and sins can be transferred to another sinner who will be punished for my sins to pay the price for me in my place. If you wrong me, on the judgment day, I can take some of my sins and [have them] transferred to you. Now, that is problematic for the Christian, but it is my understanding of what is taught in Islam. In Christianity, however, my bad deeds and sins can be transferred to a sinless Savior who was punished for my sins, who paid the price for my sins.

He had no sins to pay for because He was without sin, so He can pay the price for my sins. Likewise, in Islam, I can receive someone else's good deeds right before the Day of Judgment, right before my good and bad deeds are weighed. I can receive someone else's good deeds and righteousness in my account and be rewarded for good deeds that I never did. In Christianity, however, I can receive a sinless Savior's good deeds and His righteousness in my account to be rewarded for the good deeds that I never did. This idea in Islam that you can have a substitution, that someone can be punished for someone else's sins, I think is actually built into the whole judgment day of Islam—you can transfer your good deeds or bad deeds to someone else who you may have done wrong to or who has done wrong to you.

Again, I think the evidence is overwhelming. Jesus was a prophet of God. We have His prophecies—we know what He prophesied; they were fulfilled, they did come true, that Jesus Christ is the Savior of the world. For this cause, He came, for this cause He died, to save His people from their sins. Thank you [applause].

Ezra: James Walker. Can I have both presenters move your chairs up here? We're going to cross-examination. There will be ten minutes each, and I will let Khalil decide who goes first. You want James to go first?

Kahlil: Yes.

Ezra: He didn't have to.

Khalil: It's okay.

Ezra: Okay. I will notify you at the five-minute and two-minute mark. Mr. Walker, if you begin, please, ten minutes.

Walker: Yes. Khalil, can someone be a prophet of God without any prophecies? And if so, what could Jesus prophesy? Or if not, rather, what did Jesus prophesy?

Khalil: Can someone be a prophet without prophecy?

Walker: Without prophesying.

Khalil: I'm not sure I understand the definition of those words, but no. Jesus prophesied about the coming of Muhammad, He taught people about the oneness of God, He confirmed the Torah. He confirmed the law, and He lifted some of the restrictions that the Jews had—made it easier for them.

James: Do you believe that the Scriptures, the Old and New Testaments, were corrupted? And if so, when?

Khalil: I believe that we—that's a tough question, because I came to Islam through the Scriptures, because I thought the Bible ordered me to follow the prophet Muhammad, and I think that Jesus never claimed to be God and He never said, "I am God, worship Me." When I was trying to convert Muslims, I referred back to the Bible, and it convinced me that I was wrong. Based on that argument, I acknowledge the strength of the Bible's credibility. Since I've been a Muslim, I've heard all the arguments, and it's not just from Islam, because Christianity's vicious to itself.

If you read the apologetics of Christians, you'll find, Did Moses write the first five books [of the Bible—the books] of Genesis, Exodus, Leviticus, Numbers, and Deuteronomy? It's not a Muslim argument. We may accept the apologetics or we may not, but it's not a Muslim-unique argument…[the Injil] is talking about the Muslim life—we believe that the Injil is spoken [in] the Qur'an very clearly, we believe that Jesus delivered the Injil, the good news.

What was the good news that He gave? Well, we have Matthew, Mark, Luke, John, the letters of Paul, all of the New Testament—there's no Gospel of Jesus. There is no Injil, the words of Jesus. It's everybody quoting Jesus in their Scripture. So it's very difficult for a Muslim to understand the New Testament perspective of the Injil because it's according to 10,000 manuscripts of Matthew, Mark, Luke, and John, each and no two are identical, but they agree with each other.

We just say, "Convince me." It doesn't matter to us if they're right or wrong, but we believe that Jesus did speak the truth—that He was very clear in what He said. That He came as a messenger, a prophet—He clearly stated His objective, and He clearly told His followers that there was good news. Not Him dying on the cross for their sins, but someone who would come after Him and guide them to further truth.

James: The prophecies I recited—I think I hit all four [of] the Gospels—where they quote Jesus making prophecies about His death, His burial, His resurrection three days later: Would that be the corrupted part?

Khalil: It's confusing because the apologetics are endless, and [they] can bring up many verses and let you explain them, but it's your cross-examination, so I'll let you control your own debate. But I would just say that the Bible is very difficult [unless] you were to write down definitions of words, hold your meanings consistent throughout the Bible. Let's have a dictionary first and let's use that dictionary for the Bible. I don't care what you put in it. But let's just hold those words to meanings, and then hold those meanings to the Bible. If you do that, the apologetics of Christians gets less difficult.

James: Of course. You hear me say—

Khalil: The only reason I say that is you obviously understand that God had sons by the ton in the Bible. All of those sons were not the Son of God, even though it seems to be the sons of God. And Jesus is the Son of God, but we capitalize that one—we've referred to it in a different tense, in a different way. When we say "son," we don't mean "Son" because sonship has a definition, and it negates being divine. *Sonship*, by definition, means "to be sired, brought about somehow, fathered," and yet divine nature cannot have that. By definition, you can't be the Son of God because you are the Creator, and you have no ability to have that relationship to yourself.

So words have to have meanings, and when they do become meaningful, then the whole [Christian] concept loses all meaning.

James: You would agree, though, that Jesus was the son of Mary, although that does not imply any kind of sexual union. But [you would agree] He was literally the son of Mary?

Khalil: Yes.

James: Can you explain again why there's difficulty in saying that Jesus is the Son of God, but not that He's the son of Mary?

Khalil: Because God is divine and Mary is not. Sonship excludes divine nature. You can't be a divine son because if you're divine, you have no beginning, no end. You can't be sired, you can't be brought about, you can't be [any]one's son. If you're divine, you can't be a son to anything.

James: Does that get back to the tawhid oneness?

Khalil: Language, just [the] meanings of words.

James: You do agree, though, that Muhammad was told [when] in doubt to go to the people of the book and look at those Scriptures. He was talking about the Jews and the Christians, and apparently the Old Testament and New Testament—the Scriptures that came before, the prophets that came before. Why was he instructed to do that if [Scripture] was corrupted?

Khalil: I don't think that this issue is as big as we make it out to be. I can give you a Bible, tell you to read it, and have no preconceived theology around it. I guarantee you wouldn't come out of it with a Trinitarian view [after] just reading through it. You might, but if I give you the Old Testament and say, "Read this, and predict what's going to happen next," and all the Jews came in here and told you what all those verses meant, and you told us what some of them meant, no Jew is going to agree with your interpretation of any of those verses, and they'll call them [the verses] authentic. They'll agree with you on the authenticity of the Old Testament, but none of them—[crosstalk]

James: Some of them. Jesus and the apostles—

Khalil: I'm telling you that there's a whole lot of Jews today who have a lot of scholarship and what they believe and how they believe it, and they'll take the same exact texts that you have and they will not interpret them to mean Savior of the world, and coming for your sins in Isaiah 53. If you sit down with a Jewish rabbi and have that conversation, he is not going to come to that conclusion with you, right?

James: I have. Correct.

Khalil: I don't want to get into that, but I'm just telling you that you have a conclusion, and you impose it on the words. If you don't impose it, the Bible can read [clear]. I became a Muslim because of the Bible. I didn't read the Qur'an to become a Muslim. I didn't talk to a Muslim to become Muslim. I read the Bible, and it convinced me that Muhammad was a prophet, and that I should be a Muslim.

James: Weren't you on your way to being a Baptist preacher?

Khalil: Yes.

James: Maybe you could say that for the last question—tell me about that.

Ezra: Two minutes.

Khalil: I tried to convert a Muslim. I was in college at the University of North Texas in Denton. I was studying in my senior year. I was in [for] a degree in investment finance. I was specializing in interest rates, and I had lost all desire to do any of that. I decided I want[ed] to be a Baptist preacher; I'd grown up in a Christian family. I believed in Christianity, and I was more excited about getting back to my roots and not pursuing what I'd been in school for. Instead of throwing my education away, I decided to finish my senior year, then go to seminary.

For my entertainment, I dragged everybody around me into religious conversations. It was at that point I was asking [people], "What do you believe, and why? What do you believe, and why?" In my head, I was thinking of how I was going to preach Christianity to each person. I was preparing myself. Well, I met a Muslim, and I knew nothing—I mean, I didn't know anything good or bad about Islam. This was back in 1988. When he explained Islam to me, it took five to ten minutes; I listen[ed]. I concluded he was a confused Christian.

After I understood what he was trying to tell me, I was like, "You're a confused Christian," but this was as close as I got. Atheist, agnostic, Buddhist, Hindu, different Christians—they were…all just different emotional responses. He was almost there, and I'm like, "This Muslim thing—I don't know anything about it, but you sound like a confused Christian. I can help you." I took it upon myself to save my Muslim friend before I graduated, and here I am.

James: It didn't work. [laughs]

Khalil: Here I am.

James: Thank you.

Ezra: Khalil, ten minutes.

Khalil: James, you mentioned the verses that make your point very clear—or at least as strong as you can make it—from the biblical point of view that Jesus died on the cross and He was somehow our vicarious atonement for our sins. I'm assuming that you would agree with the Trinitarian concept of God, even the monotheistic God the Father, the Son, and the Holy Ghost. As the triune God, [they are] three in one—not three Gods, but co-eternal...what's the third one?

James: Co-eternal, co-existing.

Khalil: Okay, but [they are] totally the same, right? They're not unique, because if they're unique, they're not equal. Would you agree?

James: One true God, three distinct—*distinct* might be a better term. Distinct persons.

Khalil: Okay, so what does the word *distinct* mean?

James: Not the same person.

Khalil: We have three persons: person, person, person. Unique, unique, unique. They are the same person.

James: The same God.

Khalil: So, God is three people in one God?

James: Three whos, one what.

Khalil: The reason I highlight this is if you take that concept and just work with it, it leads to statements in the Bible making no sense. When Jesus says, "My God, My God, why has Thou forsaken Me?" the Christian answer is that He has to be one hundred percent human and one hundred percent divine. What does one hundred percent mean? That means nothing at this point, because we have to throw language out to have a conversation. So when He said the Father is greater than I, and we are equal, those two terms don't mix: greater than, and equal.

James: Is that a question?

Khalil: I'm getting all of them and you can just...

James: Okay.

Khalil: Because they are all going to be [the] same apologetic. I'm assuming, so I'm doing all instead of one by one so you can come back because they all are one. Jesus said, "The Father is greater than I; I of mine own self did nothing." "Why callest me good, there is none good but the Father, our Father who art in heaven?" "My God, My God why has Thou forsaken Me?" In ample places, He is just bluntly telling you that God is the one who deserves your worship and that it is not Him [Jesus]. "I don't know the hour; I don't know the time; I don't know anything. I am not the person that you need to be coming to for this information; I'm like you." When He was saying that, He was trying to tell everybody very clearly that He was here to guide them to that Father, to that God, to that person, to that entity, whatever you want to call it. And that is the same thing Moses did, the same thing Abraham did, the same thing Muhammad did. That there is no way to get to this person unless you listen to what I'm telling you.

In Islam, we say, "Laa ilaaha"—there is no God but Allah, and Muhammad is the messenger of God. But before Muhammad it was "Laa ilaaha"—there is no God, and ʿĪsa is the messenger of God, or Moses is the messenger of God, or Abraham is the messenger of God—so they were very clear on what they said, and yet we single out Jesus [and] say no, He was totally different. But the Jews disagree with you, and the Muslims disagree with you, and yet

Christians just carve out this niche and say, "No, all words changed to mean what we need it to mean."

James: I don't think it changes the meaning so much—maybe sometimes it's a misunderstanding, maybe we are not communicating clearly what we're trying to say on that. There is a difference between being equal in deity, in divinity, and then in the area of authority. For example, the Bible says women are to be in submission to their husbands, and most of the time, my wife is in submission to me. That doesn't mean that I'm more human than she is, or she is subhuman and I'm superhuman. We are equally human in God's sight, equally loved by God, yet the wife is to be in submission to the husband.

You see that also in our history in the United States. We have two presidents—George Bush is ironically a father and a son. When the father was the president of the United States, who was greater than the other? The father was greater; he was president of the United States. The son—maybe he owned the Texas Rangers at the time, I'm not sure—would say the father is greater than the son positionally, yes. But in their humanity, they are equally human. The son is not subhuman, the father is not superhuman.

Khalil: But they are two humans.

James: Exactly—

Khalil: You are not saying two gods.

James: Jesus being equally God, right?

Khalil: No.

James: But voluntary submission—

Khalil: What is a God?

James: This is another [place where] I think there is a misunder-standing—the words *voluntary submission* are seen as [referring to] inferiority. But Jesus told His disciples, "If you want to be the great-est, let Me tell you how to do it: Be the servant." He demonstrated that by His greatness, by how great of a servant He was. This doesn't mean He was inferior; that's a sign of Jesus's way of superiority.

Khalil: What did Jesus say His greatest miracle was?

James: I'm not sure what His greatest miracle…

Khalil: He says it in the Bible.

James: Okay, what is the text?

Khalil: He says, "As Jonah was in the belly of the big fish for three days and three nights, the Son of Man be in the belly of the earth for three days and three nights," right? He said that was His greatest miracle. Okay. How was Jonah in the belly of the fish: alive or dead?

James: Well, I'm assuming he was alive.

Khalil: Okay; so did Jonah die?

James: You can find the parallels, the symbolism there. You are not saying—

Khalil: Again, if I want to interpret the whole Bible my way, it's easy. I can pick the [meanings] and make you a Muslim in a sense that makes my argument clear. You can make your argument from the same verses [so] you're clear. The audience can hear both sides and make their choice.

How much time for my questions?

Ezra: Three-and-a-half minutes.

Khalil: What sin, in Christianity, does God the Father forgive?

James: Which sin does He forgive?

Khalil: Give me any sin that He forgives.

James: Murder. You mean can God forgive murder?

Khalil: Yes. Okay. How does He do that?

James: Through the atonement of Jesus Christ.

Khalil: What is the atonement? Is that a payment?

James: That's part of what it means, yes.

Khalil: If you pay for sin, are you forgiven?

James: If that payment is received, yes. If it's applied to your account, yes.

Khalil: Okay. So if I pay a traffic ticket, is that the same as the court forgiving me and not making me pay?

James: If the court accepts that payment.

Khalil: No. Can a judge just tell me, "Khalil don't pay the ticket. I forgive you?" That's the kind of advice I'm looking at, right?

James: A judge could do that. Yes.

Khalil: Okay.

James: An unrighteous judge, yes.

Khalil: So God cannot forgive anything in that sense, that He demands payment for everything in Christianity—

James: He could forgive, but the scales still have to be balanced in Muslim terms.

Khalil: No, I'm asking a straightforward question. The word *forgive* means not to collect if you owe me something. I forgive the debt. I do not expect you to pay. Is that correct?

James: Yes.

Khalil: So you owe me $100, and I say, "James, I forgive you; do not pay me." Okay, then I've forgiven the debt. I don't want to collect it. All right. That's what I mean by forgiveness. What sin does God forgive?

James: All sin can be forgiven.

Khalil: Uncollected.

James: Well, God chooses to pay because He's a righteous judge.

Khalil: That means He excludes forgiveness. Those are mutually exclusive: either you pay, or forgive, or neither. But if you do one, you exclude the other. So when I pay you, there's no forgiveness. When there's forgiveness, there's no payment. They are mutually exclusive, one or the other. Which sin does God forgive?

James: God forgives by making the payment for me.

Khalil: That's collection. That's not forgiveness.

James: Maybe that's one of the terminology differences that we have.

Khalil: Then what's the word for forgiveness? In other words, to not collect. I am a sinner. I'm the guilty party. My God can forgive me or He can collect. So one of the two: He can punish, or forgive.

A Muslim can ask for forgiveness; God says, "Ask, and you shall receive." Right? So you ask for forgiveness. He can forget it. He gives it to anyone who asks. So His justice is absolutely the same for every human being at all times, 24/7, till the Day of Judgment.

So it is perfect justice in that you commit a crime, you're guilty. You ask for forgiveness, you will get it until the Day of Judgment. So the justice is 100 percent just, because the forgiveness is 100 percent available 24 hours a day, seven days a week, 365 days a year, until your death. So if He wants to hold you accountable, He can punish you. If He wants to forgive you, He can forgive you. If He forgives, He doesn't collect. If He collects, He doesn't forgive. My God has mercy, has kindness, can forgive sins. And He can do it for anybody. It's not me, it's not arbitrary, it's not capricious. It's upon request. So anyone and everyone has access to that 24/7 until they're dead.

James: Was that true, false, or multiple choice?

Khalil: I'm asking you if you have any concept of forgiveness in Christianity like this?

James: Can I answer?

Ezra: Last response, yes.

James: Short answer to that, yes. We believe that the wages of sin is death, that this is a standard, this is in accordance with God's holiness and righteousness. And He would be an unjust God to say, "I know I said that, but I was just kidding. [The penalty] doesn't have to be death. You don't worry about it." Now you may have a grandfatherly judge who would do that on a traffic ticket or something like that. But let's say there's a murder case and the judge decides to let the person go. There are a lot of family members of those victims who will say, "That's not just; that's not a just judge doing that." So in Christianity, the justice is satisfied completely because Jesus saves your—

Khalil: So there is no forgiveness.

James: He forgives by making the payment for you.

Khalil: Words don't have any meaning. You're back to words that have no meaning. There is no forgiveness in Christianity; there's zero forgiveness. Jesus paid for all sins, paid [them] in full. Complete. Absolute. There is zero forgiveness; there's nothing forgiven. It's all collected.

Ezra: Thank you.

Khalil: And in fact, I would encourage all of us, to me included, go whatever direction—it doesn't really matter; be honest with yourself. That's the best advice I can give myself, James, or you: Whatever you believe, believe it! For God's sake, believe it. Sink your life into it.

Believe it, trust it, and as you go down whatever path that is, be sincere with yourself. Don't lie to yourself. Do not get to a point where no matter what happens you are going to lie to yourself. If you're honest with yourself, then either you weren't capable of understanding something, or God will accept whatever you believe because you're sincere in your belief. I believe that there's only one truth; I don't think they are all true, but God will hold you accountable to your sincerity and to your effort.

So if you do nothing and say, "Well, I'm going to stay on the couch and I'm right," then that arrogance, or whatever it is, whether you're right or wrong, is a choice you're making. For me, I'm going to keep learning and listening and telling people what I have. If I see something better, I'm going to have to ask myself, "Yes or no?" That's all there is.

God is going to hold you accountable for your sincerity and your effort, right? And that combination is different for all of us.

Ezra: Closing statements, although I think that was a really good one.

Khalil: I'm good; go ahead.

Ezra: James—closing statement.

James: Again, to make my case that Jesus Christ is both the prophet of God and the Savior of the world, I think there is very compelling evidence for that. Every extant copy of every first-century Gospel that we have affirms this. Every writing of His closest followers affirms it. Every early church father confesses it. Every eyewitness account agrees. Every prophecy by the earlier prophets don't contradict and they affirm. Every prophecy by Jesus Himself affirms this.

So we could argue, "Oh, maybe the Gospels have been corrupted, or maybe the Gospel of Jesus has nothing to do with Matthew, Mark, Luke, and John." We don't have anything from the first century that looks like the Qur'an, so therefore we don't have access to it, but if you're going to say that Jesus had followers and beliefs and gospels and teachings, if you have something totally different than everything that we have in print, everything that we have extant, everything that we have right now, you [would] think that you would have very compelling evidence for [what you say].

And this leads me to the Day of Judgment. From my perspective, the Muslim has no Savior. In my mind, this is the fatal flaw of Islam: You're standing alone, standing naked as a sinner before a holy, righteous God, the judge of the universe, the creator of the universe—you're standing before Him.

It's not just me saying this. Let me take you to answering-christianity.com.

Khalil: You are not putting words in my mouth; go right ahead.

James: Your belief in the one true living God almighty and your good deeds—

Khalil: I did not say my good deeds do me any good. That did not come out of my mouth.

James: No, I'm talking about answering-christianity.com, a popular Muslim website. Your belief in the one true living God almighty and your good deeds are your savior in Islam. In Islam—

Khalil: Your belief is all that saves you.

James: In Islam, you don't need for anyone to die for your sins; I think you would affirm that.

Khalil: I agree with that.

James: [Muslims say] we don't believe in mediators between the creator and the creation—in Islam, you have a direct relationship with Allah almighty. [Muslims say] I don't need anyone to die for my sins. We [Muslims and Christians] also believe in the Day of Judgment. I want to end in the area of firm agreement.

Khalil: One hundred percent.

James: The atheists who are up on the stage don't, but we agree on this. We will look at two judgments, which we call the Bema Judgment, the Great White Throne Judgment. I just want to deal with the Great White Throne Judgment for just a second. The book of Revelation, Revelation 20: "I saw the dead, great and small, standing before the throne, and the books were opened—notice the plural—and the books were opened, then another book—notice the singular—was opened, which is the book of life." Sometimes called the Lamb's book of life. This is the book where [the names of] all the saved are written down, the ones who trust Christ as their Savior.

Khalil: The ones who believe in God only.

James: Yes. "And the dead were judged by what was written in the books according to what they had done." Guess how many make it to salvation when they're judged by the books plural? "If anyone's name was not found written in the Book of Life—that's singular—he was thrown into the Lake of Fire."

What we see is that everyone who was judged by the things that they had done, none of them made it. They were all thrown in the Lake of Fire. There is nothing about a good deed offsetting a bad deed, or Allah putting his thumb on the side of the good deed. We don't have that. You don't want to be judged by the things you've done; you want your name to be in the book singular.

I want to end with one final prophecy of Jesus. He prophesied about me and you; He prophesied about our future. Here's His prophecy, this is John 8:24: "I told you that you would die in your sins, for unless you believe that I am He"—this in the Greek is *ego eimi*, a direct quote of the Septuagint, Exodus 3, the burning bush, where Moses asked, "Who is it? What is your name?" *Ego eimi.*

"If you do not believe that I am He"—*ego eimi*—"you will die in your sins." So this is why it is extremely important, from our perspective, and this is why it's my heart's desire (and I know your heart's desire is for me to be Muslim) and prayer is that you, my friend Khalil, would also know Jesus not just as a prophet of God, but also as the Savior of the world, and your Savior.

Khalil: Thank you.

Ezra: Thank you all. James Walker, Khalil Meek [applause].

A Personal Illustration:
Obey Jesus?

In the next three chapters, you'll read interviews I did with former Muslims who made the journey from Islam to Christianity. Before we get into the interviews, I would like to share about an interesting encounter I had a few years ago.

I was sitting in a Starbucks coffee shop when a man entered the door and I noticed two things: First, he had an Islamic dictionary with him, so I assumed he was a Muslim. Second, I realized that there was only one empty seat left in the shop—right next to me.

I had been reading the Bible on my iPad, but as he approached, I quickly switched to the Qur'an. I never said anything to him, but a few minutes later, he tapped me on the shoulder and pointed to my iPad. He smiled warmly and said, "You must be Muslim; you are reading the Qur'an." I smiled back and said, "Yes, I am reading the Qur'an, but I am actually Christian."

His smile was replaced by a look of confusion. He asked, "But why would you be reading the Qur'an?" I answered that while I did not believe the Qur'an to be scripture, I thought it was important to know what it teaches and what Muslims believe.

I told him that I was having difficulty understanding parts of the Qur'an. He said, "I am a Muslim; I will help you understand."

I then read Surah 3:50 to him. There, Jesus says you must "fear Allah and obey me."

My new friend said, "Yes, you must fear Allah and obey Jesus. This is what we believe."

"My confusion," I said, "is how do we obey Jesus without knowing His commands? I am unable to locate any of Jesus's commandments anywhere in the Qur'an."

He reached over, took my iPad out of my hands, and began reading the whole chapter, looking for a list of Jesus's commandments. After a few minutes, he sighed and said, "I am not a scholar of the Qur'an, so I cannot locate the commands of Jesus. But I have friends who are experts in the Qur'an. I will ask them to give me the list."

I thanked him for his willingness to help me, and our conversation drifted to topics of a nonspiritual nature.

I had almost forgotten about the conversation until I saw him again about a week later in the same Starbucks. I smiled at him and waved at him across the room. He smiled back, got up, and came over to join me.

We talked about other things for quite a while, then I asked, "Hey, remember we discussed the commands of Jesus? You were going to check with your scholar friends to get me a list of them from the Qur'an."

He smiled again and said, "Oh yes," but then he lowered his head and said, "No, they could not find the commands of Jesus either."

I replied, "I was thinking about that. Where else could we find the commands of Jesus except in the Gospels—Matthew, Mark, Luke, and John?"

He said, "Oh no, my friend. The Gospels have been corrupted."

I said, "But where else can we find Jesus's commandments? Do you think there is anything of value in the Gospels?"

He answered, "I don't know...I don't think so."

I asked, "Can I ask you, my friend, if have you ever read the Gospels? For example, have you ever read Matthew's Gospel?"

He answered, "No, they are not in my language. I am from Pakistan."

He seemed to have a good grasp of English, but evidently this was a big issue to him. I asked, "What is your language?"

"I speak Urdu."

I said, "I have a feeling that Matthew's Gospel may be available in Urdu." I did a quick search on my iPad, then handed it to him—with Matthew's Gospel in Urdu on the screen.

"My friend," I asked, "if I brought you a printed copy, would you be willing to read the Gospel of Matthew with me in Urdu so we could discuss any commands of Jesus that we discover?"

He looked directly at me and his eyes narrowed slightly. As a small smile spread across his lips, he said, "No! Instead, we make a deal. I will read this Matthew, but you must agree to read Qur'an Surah 2 and Surah 19."

I laughed out loud at that, shook his hand, and said, "Deal!"

One week later, we met at Starbucks again. I had brought a copy of the Gospel of Matthew with me. I was even able to snap a picture of the first time he was able to read the Gospel in his heart language.

That gift copy of the Gospel of Matthew opened the door for many other great gospel conversations. We were able to talk about the commands of Jesus that he read in Matthew, and how they compared with the commands of Allah found in the Qur'an. We discussed the Day of Judgment and his lack of assurance that his sins have been forgiven.

As of today, he has not made that transition from Islam to embrace Jesus as his Savior. He has, however, shown a real awareness of the differences between the Qur'an and the Bible. He has also asked questions that lead me to believe he is beginning to grasp the central message of the Christian gospel. Please pray that in the days to come, Jesus will reveal His grace and that my friend will come to truly know what it means to "obey Jesus."

> He who believes in the Son has eternal life; but he who does not obey the Son will not see life, but the wrath of God abides on him (John 3:36).

Chapter 16

Interview with Zia Hassan, Former Sunni Muslim

Zia Hassan is a former Sunni Muslim from Pakistan. In this interview, he shares the remarkable story of his devout Muslim background followed by troubling doubts that eventually led him on a journey from the religion of Islam to Jesus of the Bible.

Note: *The interviews in chapters 17–19 have had minor edits made to them for brevity and clarity.*

James: Zia, tell me a bit about your Muslim background.

Zia: I'm originally from Pakistan, and I was born in a very devout Sunni family, and all my family members back home are still practicing Sunnis. I came to the United States in 1984. The last six to seven years, I was still a devout Muslim, and I was going every single Friday to mosque, and saying a prayer in my mosque.

James: And that was both in Pakistan and when you first came to the United States?

Zia: Yes, it was a little more in Pakistan because I knew that I was surrounded by all my relatives and brothers and sisters. I had no choice but to go to the mosque.

James: I know that the Qur'an talks about Jesus. What were you taught? What did you believe about Jesus as a Muslim?

Zia: What the Qur'an teaches about Jesus and what we believe are totally different. What we were taught by the Imams—or our mom and dad—is that Jesus, or 'Isa, is a holy prophet of Allah, one of the prophets. They believe that there are 124,000 prophets in Islam, and 'Isa is one of them. That's all we were taught—that He's a holy prophet, and nothing else. But when I studied the Qur'an, then I found out totally different things about the Jesus.

James: When you studied the Qur'an, did you learn things about Jesus that you never knew otherwise?

Zia: Correct.

James: What were some of those things?

Zia: The number one thing I learned when I studied the Qur'an is that Jesus was born from the virgin Mary, and the spirit of Allah, which is called *Ru-Allah*, and that He is also called Word of Allah.

James: Was this something the Imams did not teach, and you did not learn until you read the Qur'an for yourself?

Zia: I heard it mentioned when I came to United States; the Imam used to talk about that in the mosque. When I was a practicing Muslim, we were told you cannot be a good Muslim if you don't believe in Jesus Christ, or 'Isa ibn Maryam. Both refer to the same person, but with totally different meanings. When you ask the Imams questions that are a little bit more in-depth, then you find out what they believe. But to answer your question, yes, the Qur'an does teach about Ru-Allah, which is the spirit of God, and also about the word of Allah, or *kalimatim-minallaah*, which is "a Word from God." As I studied the Qur'an more, I found out that He has divine attributes.

Ten or eleven years ago, I stopped studying the Qur'an in the language I understand—I don't understand Arabic. I still memorized the Qur'an, but I didn't understand the meaning of the verses I was reading. The Qur'an clearly talks about Jesus Christ, that He's totally different than the other prophets. His birth was unique, He was born of the virgin Mary and Spirit of God, He was the Word of God, and He was performing miracles that no other human could do—only God could do them. When I read those verses, I thought, *Wait a minute—this is not just another prophet. No other prophet has done what He did. No other prophet has given life to a dead person. No other prophet has given eyesight to a blind person except for this one. He is different. Why?*

That was an intriguing question for me, and I was curious. I wanted to know more, so I studied more.

James: So the Jesus in the Qur'an was born of a virgin?

Zia: That's correct.

James: Is there any other prophet in Islam—

Zia: No other prophet was born like that. He is mentioned in Qur'an, believe it or not, twenty-five times—He is called *'Isa ibn Maryam*. One other thing I would like to point out is that when I read the Arabic term used to refer to Him, *Masih*, for a while I did not realize the meaning of the term, which is "Christ." I went to Google to find out what *Christ* means—"the anointed one."

James: That is Messiah—

James: That reading in the Qur'an is not in Arabic. Are you reading it in your language?

Zia: Every Muslim has to read the Qur'an in Arabic first, because it is said that Arabic is the language of Allah. But to understand the

Qur'an, I read and study it in English. That helps me to have a better understanding.

James: So what the Qur'an says about Jesus is more unique than what it says about any other prophet, including Muhammad. What does the Qur'an say about Jesus being the Son of God?

Zia: That's another thing. If you're Muslim, there is a prayer you say five times a day. This is what devout Muslims are supposed to do. Every Muslim has to recite this prayer from the Qur'an:

> Qul huwal laahu ahad.
> Allah hus-samad
> Lam yalid wa lam yoolad
> Wa lam yakul-lahu kufuwan ahad.

Basically, this prayer says that God is not a father, and He didn't have a son. He does not have a begotten son. You have to say this prayer every day. It is from the Qur'an, which clearly denies that Jesus Christ was the Son of God. That's what I used to believe. Muslims believe the only way you can have a son or daughter is by sexual intercourse between a wife and husband. But we know He was not the result of sexual union, so we don't see how He is the Son. So to answer your question, yes. Muslims totally deny that Jesus is the Son of God.

James: It's interesting to note that throughout the Qur'an, we read that Jesus was the son of Mary.

Zia: Correct.

James: But they think that is not at all sexual. So you can be the son of someone—

Zia: Yes.

James: —but without there being an allegation of a sexual contact.

Zia: Yes.

James: There's another big difference between what we find in the Gospels and in the Qur'an. What does the Qur'an say about Jesus being God, or God in the flesh, the incarnation?

Zia: There's no such thing that Jesus Christ is God almighty in human flesh. To say that is the biggest sin you could commit. And, you know, a Muslim can't even think about it. If you even start thinking about this idea, you've already committed a sin. There's no such thing in the Qur'an. If you ever get a chance to look at the Dome of the Rock in the Middle East, there are words on the Dome of the Rock that clearly deny Christianity.

It says clearly in the Qur'an—I think it's Surah 4:171—there is no Son of God. So the Qur'an is totally the opposite of Christianity. After studying this, I found out that Christianity answers your questions. Christianity speaks of Jesus Christ and His death on the cross and His resurrection on the third day. The Qur'an denies both. And there is no Christianity if there is no resurrection.

The Qur'an doesn't say that Jesus died on the cross. There was somebody else whom God chose for that—someone died, but it wasn't Jesus. However, the Qur'an does say that no other prophet has done all the miracles Jesus did. No other prophet came back to life and went to heaven except Jesus Christ. Those are the unique things about Jesus. He is the only one who went back into heaven. No other prophets did that.

James: So, the Qur'an says that Jesus didn't die on the cross. Does it say what happened to Jesus?

Zia: Yes. They said there was the Surah Al-Nisa [Surah 4:157]. It says that [the Jews or Pharisees claimed to have crucified Him but the Qur'an says of Jesus] "they killed him not." It appears to them—maybe somebody else looked like Him [was crucified in His place]. Allah took Jesus to heaven before they crucified him, and he picked him up and took him to heaven and put some other innocent man on the cross. So it only appeared to them that Jesus was killed. But according to Islam, Jesus was not crucified.

James: It was a case of mistaken identity?

Zia: No, not a mistaken identity. The best way I can put it is that Allah deceived everybody. Allah deceived all the Christians and the entire world. Christians believe that Jesus was crucified; Allah deceived them. It wasn't Jesus on the cross; Allah took Him up to heaven. Muslims are very clear on that.

James: Are there any theories about who went to the cross instead of Jesus?

Zia: Some might say it was Judas, the disciple who deceived Jesus Christ. They say maybe it was him. But there's no clear indication of that.

James: That's interesting.

Zia: Yeah.

James: When you were a Muslim, were you ever encouraged to think it was possible to have a close spiritual relationship with Jesus?

Zia: Oh, absolutely not. No way. We're not supposed to read the Bible. We're not even supposed to touch it. To do that is to commit a sin. We're supposed to read the Qur'an, not the Bible. We are also told not to ask questions. There is no teaching that we can have a spiritual relationship with Jesus Christ. We are to obey the God called Allah.

James: Is the one true God of Islam, Allah, in some ways unknowable or untouchable or distant and separate?

Zia: Correct. Islam teaches, "There's one God that's the same." The God of Adam, Isaac, Abraham—that is Allah. But when I started studying, I realized there's a huge difference between Allah and the God of Christianity. They are totally different. As I was studying the Qur'an more in Arabic, I was totally shocked by what I found out about Allah.

James: Although the Qur'an calls Jesus Messiah, do Muslims see Him as being the Savior of the world?

Zia: No. They call Him a Messiah, but not knowingly. They don't understand what *Messiah* means. They don't believe He is the Savior. They believe on their good deeds and bad deeds.

I asked my Imam Muslim friends, "Do you consider yourself better than Adam? Adam was a prophet." They say Adam was a prophet, but because he made one simple, lousy mistake, he was kicked out of the presence of God almighty. I tell my friends, "God and sin—or mistake, or whatever we want to call it—cannot coexist. Do you consider yourself better than Adam?" They say, "No." I say, "If Adam got kicked out of heaven for one mistake, how many good deeds do you think you have to do to get back into the presence of God or in heaven?"

My friends have no answer for that. Muslims also don't believe in original sin. But the reason we are all living on Earth is because Allah kicked Adam out and made him dwell on Earth. We are here on Earth today because of someone else's mistake—someone else's original sin.

There is no spiritual relationship. Instead, Muslims try to use their good deeds to get back to God. They try to do as many good deeds as they can.

James: As a Muslim, what did you think was going to happen on the Day of Judgment?

Zia: Muslims believe Muhammad will be there on the Day of Judgment. If your good deeds outweigh your bad deeds, you will go to heaven. The good deeds could include performing the five times of prayer or salat each day. You can also fast, or do sawm. You can perform hajj, or go to Saudi Arabia at least once during your lifetime. These are among the five pillars of Islam. Of course you have to do shahada ["There is no god but Allah, and Muhammad is the messenger of Allah."]. Your religious rituals and good deeds have to outweigh the bad deeds.

James: As a Muslim, did you ever come to a place where you felt like you had done enough good deeds so that you had no need to fear the Day of Judgment?

Zia: According to Qur'an, I can't have an opinion about that. The Qur'an says that even the prophet Muhammad did not know whether he was saved, or what was going to happen to him. I ask my loved one, "Do you know how much he had to have done?" No one knows.

Two years ago when I went home, I asked my brother and sister, "When you go to sleep, do you know where you will be headed if you don't wake up again? Are you going to end up in heaven?" They answered, "I sure hope so." Even the very religious people who have performed all the good deeds don't know the answer. All they can say is, "I sure hope so." There's no assurance of salvation in Islam.

James: In Islam, Jesus is not the Savior of the world. Is there a savior? Who is that savior?

Zia: There is no savior. Muslims don't believe in anyone as savior. You have to do it on your own. You have to perform, you have to do things yourself to get to God. There's no concept of a savior in Islam.

James: Can you tell me, Zia, about your transition from Islam to Christianity? What started this? How did you become interested? Take us on your journey from Islam to Christianity.

Zia: I have a long answer and a short answer. The short answer is my questions, my curiosity. I was asking, "Why this? Why that?" That's what happened to me. Twelve to fourteen years ago, my son Michael passed away. Now, be aware I helped to pioneer the building of two mosques in my hometown. When I took my son's body to a Christian cemetery, I asked an Imam to come say the prayer. As he came over to me, he whispered in my ear, "Hey, brother, don't bury your son in a Christian cemetery; God will punish him until the Day of Judgment." He said that because I was going to bury my innocent child in a Christian cemetery. I was upset; I was devastated by his comment. I asked myself, *Why did he say that? Where did this come from? Was this his own opinion, or was this from the Qur'an?* That opened my eyes. At the time, I had no desire to accept Christianity because I had been brainwashed against it. I had no desire to learn anything else; I just wanted to study my own faith.

Every time I read the Qur'an, I said, "Wait a minute, that's what I believe." Then finally I said, "No, no that's not what I believe," or "I don't know." As a Muslim, you have to accept the Qur'an one hundred percent. You cannot cherry pick—you cannot say, "I don't like this verse here." Either you accept it or you reject it, period. And I said, "No, I don't believe this stuff."

I used to facilitate Christian apologists and Muslim apologists to debate back in the early 1990s. I used to hear from my Muslim brothers that Jesus Christ isn't mentioned in the Bible; that's what we were taught. I said, "I'm going find out for myself." I didn't believe anyone; I didn't trust anyone. I said, "I'm going to study the Bible. I'm going to find where Muhammad is mentioned in the Bible." But I did not have a Bible at the time.

I used to go to Barnes and Noble in the Parks Mall [in Arlington,

Texas] to study the Bible. Every time I had a day off, I went to Barnes and Noble, picked up a Bible, and read it. Muhammad was nowhere to be found. Muslims say he is mentioned in Deuteronomy 8:18 and John 4:14. But they are twisting those verses out of context. When I started reading the Bible, I thought, *Wait a minute*. I went to Matthew, and when I start reading the Sermon on the Mount, I thought, *My gosh. This is not a man speaking.* That's what got my attention to read the Bible more.

So, to answer your question, when my son passed away, I studied the Qur'an. I found I had to reject most of it. Now I completely reject it. I did not accept Christianity overnight—not by peer pressure or spouse pressure. It was my own idea to study the Bible, and I'm still doing it. For about four or five years, I studied the Bible. Then I said, "This is it." The Qur'an talks about Jesus Christ; He performed divine miracles like only God can do. I also read that God forgives sin; Jesus Christ forgives sin. Once I understood the concept of sin and how we became separated from God—once I understood that—then I had to accept Jesus Christ as my Savior and Lord.

James: Does your family know that you're a Christian?

Zia: Yes, they know, and a couple of my sisters are devastated. They had strong reactions. One sister, who was very close to me, told me a few years ago not to call her anymore. A couple of my friends who used to see me regularly at the mosque don't see me anymore. They don't associate with me. That's fine. I'm not worried about that. Rather, I am worried about my own eternity.

The cost I'm paying is nothing compared to what He paid on the cross for me. It's nothing. What He has done for me on the cross… my own cross is nothing.

James: Have your Muslim friends or family members tried to talk you out of Christianity, or tell you that Christianity is not true and that you need to come back to Islam?

Zia: Yes. In fact, that's how I approach my Muslim friends and family. I have said, "I'm giving you the chance, the opportunity, to bring me back." I have said, "You think your brother is lost? If I'm lost, bring me back. Let's have an intelligent dialogue. I'm not asking for your opinion or my opinion. Let's open the Qur'an, and you tell me if that's the truth." I'm not a scholar, but I tell them, "Don't put your destiny or eternity in somebody else's understanding. Why don't you study and understand for yourself?"

Yes, they have tried to talk with me, but when I ask them questions, they don't have any answers. In fact, one of my best friends from New York called me and said, "Hey bro, what's this?" I explained to him what I learned, and after that he said, "You're right; it's making sense." I said, "I want you to study for yourself. Don't believe what I'm saying. Study this for yourself." He is studying right now.

James: Have any of your family members taken you up on that challenge or opportunity?

Zia: No, because of where they live. They are all in Pakistan, every single one of them. As you know, there is capital punishment for those who go apostate. If you change your religion there, they chop your head off.

James: As a former Muslim who has abandoned the faith of Islam, did you feel at all in danger when you revisited your country Pakistan?

Zia: Not at all. I went back home almost two years ago, and I had no fear at all. I was very open, and about two days before I was supposed to fly out, I called all my siblings. My siblings are older than me. My older sister is seventy-three. I told them, "I'm going to take you out for lunch." While we were out, I told them, "I need to tell you something personal. I'm no longer a Muslim. I don't practice it. I have rejected the ideology."

A couple of my sisters cried out loud. I said, "Why are you crying?" One said, "I cry for you every night because I know where you are heading." Another sister just stared at me. I said, "I'm just telling you about my faith. I have rejected my ancestors' faith, my mom and dad's faith. And I have accepted Christianity because I have studied it. I have done the research." So yes, they know.

James: As a former Muslim who is now a Christian, what advice do you have for a Christian who has a Muslim neighbor or coworker or friend? How do we go about building a bridge? What advice could you share with us as Christians?

Zia: I strongly believe we have to show them love and approach them positively. Ask them, "Why do you believe as you do?" If a Muslim is eager to bring the infidel, or Christian, to Islam, the best way to approach that Muslim is to say, "I'm interested in Islam. Can you share with me what you believe? And why you believe that?" Once you engage them in conversation, then you can say, "Is this your opinion, or is this from the Qur'an?" The best way to do this is to make sure you also know their faith. You need to know what they believe before you engage yourself in conversation. That way, if they give you information that is not accurate, instead of telling them that they are wrong, you can say, "I understand what you are talking about. Do I understand this correctly, or do you need to correct me?" In this way, you can show a Muslim that you know about his faith.

That's what I do. I have a couple of friends who work with me, and when I ask them questions, they say, "I don't know the answer. You know this better than I do." I tell them, "Why don't you learn?" The best way to talk with anyone is to get to know their faith first. It doesn't matter if the person is a Mormon or Jehovah's Witness or Muslim. Once you know what they believe, you can talk with them about their beliefs. That's the best way to do it.

James: You would not recommend that a person start by overly criticizing the prophet Muhammad, or by attacking a Muslim's beliefs? You would still say it is best to start with questions?

Zia: Yes. If you start by criticizing their prophet, the conversation is finished. He or she will not talk to you because that's their man. If you insult Allah in any way, you have three days to repent and you're okay. Once you repent, you're forgiven. But [if you insult Muhammad], even if you repent they are still going to kill you because Muhammad is above you. No one is allowed to insult him. That's the criteria they use.

James: So to understand correctly, if you insult God, the sin can be forgiven. But if you insult Muhammad, even if you repent you—

Zia: You're still going to be put to death. That's exactly right…if you want to engage yourself in conversation with a Muslim, you don't go straight to Muhammad's character or to negative information about him. You want to talk about doctrine. You say, "I want to learn a doctrine. What does Islam teach about this? I'm interested. Teach me what you know." You can also ask, "How did you become a Muslim?" Muslims believe that all the prophets were Muslims, including Jesus. That's what they believe.

James: Are there Christians in Pakistan?

Zia: Yes.

James: How are they viewed?

Zia: The majority of Christians in Pakistan use the last name *Masih*. That is how they identify themselves as Christians. My name is Zia, and I write it as Zia Masih. The *Masih* speaks of the Messiah, and it is a very derogatory term back home. Only about one to two percent of the population in Pakistan are Christians. They do all the dirty work for everyone else. They're untouchable. And they are supposed to stay away from you—about five or six feet away. They come to your homes, they clean up all your dirty stuff. *Masih* is a derogatory term. The only jobs allocated to Christians are jobs that nobody else wants to do. Christians clean the streets, the toilets, you name it. And when I say toilet, I'm not talking about toilets like in America. In Pakistan, there are old-fashioned toilets that don't use a flush system. This means the Christians have to do very dirty work. It's a sad situation for the Christians in Pakistan.

James: On your last visit, did you have any encounters with one of those Christians?

Zia: Yes, I had an encounter. It was sad. I took my nephew and my brother out to eat a nice lunch. When you go to the bathroom to wash your hands, inside is an attendant who hands you a towel. As you wash your hands, you can look in the mirror and see him standing behind you, very alert. These lowly workers are brainwashed and are told that they are not worthy of anything better.

This man was standing behind me, and as I looked in the mirror, I said, "What's your name, son?" He said, "Sir, my name is Johnny Masih." I went to him and said, "I want to shake hands with you." He said, "No, sir. I'm a Christian; don't shake my hand." I said, "Come on, give me a hug." He was shocked. I said, "You don't want to shake hands with me? I want to give you a hug." Then I said, "Listen, I'm just like you." And then we talked. He started crying, and I cried too.

He said, "Sir, where are you from?" I told him about what had happened to me, and he said, "Sir, I've never heard anything like that before." I said, "You are just like me, brother. Give me a hug."

There was another encounter I had with my niece. I was visiting her home. My sister cooked us a nice lunch, and this incident happened. My niece is a professor; she's very literate, knowledgeable, and smart. We were all sitting inside, waiting for her to arrive and eat lunch with us. She was the only one not there yet. All the rest of my nieces were there, my brother was there, my wife was there, my sister was there. Then I heard someone banging on the door and not ringing the doorbell.

I asked my sister, "Is someone banging on the door?" My sister mentioned my niece's name and said, "That's her." I said, "Why is she not ringing the doorbell?" My sister replied, "She will not touch the doorbell because the *Masih*, the guy who comes and picks up the filth, pushed the doorbell with his dirty finger. That's why she will not touch the button and instead, she is banging on the door. I thought, *Oh my, does she know what I am now? What's she going do?* She came inside, and she wouldn't talk to me. She knew about my views and said, "How are you doing, Uncle?" Then she went away from me.

Yes, the situation is tragic for Christians in Pakistan. They are very miserable, and I feel sorry for them.

Chapter 17

Interview with Elijah,
Former Shia Muslim[1]

Elijah is a former Shia Muslim raised as a minority among the Sunni Muslims in Baghdad, Iraq. In this interview, he shares what it was like to grow up Shia, and the longing that he had for true forgiveness and a relationship with God. He recounts the spiritual quest that brought him out of Islam, through a false Christian conversion, and finally, to the gospel of the grace of Jesus Christ.

James: Elijah, tell me about your Muslim background.

Elijah: I grew up in Baghdad, Iraq, in a Shia Muslim family. I had a large family, lots of brothers and sisters, which is typical for a Muslim family. My parents were devout, but they did not push Islam on us, as far as how devout they were.

They encouraged us, but I grew up as a secular Muslim. Islamic teaching was taught to all of us, whether at home, or school, or through the culture, or at the mosque. In a Muslim country, Islam is everywhere. It's part of your identity. That's how I grew up.

James: What is the main difference between Shia and Sunni Muslims?

Elijah: Let me put it this way: Shia is like Catholicism. It's all about hierarchy. You've got the Ayatollah, or the lineage of Ali, which is

Muhammad's cousin and the fourth caliph, or the successor after Muhammad died.

James: The division [between Shia and Sunni] happened early on, after the death of Muhammad?

Elijah: Immediately after the death of Muhammad. There were two groups. The minority, the smaller group, wanted a bloodline from Muhammad. The only bloodline, the only survivor, because none of Muhammad's sons survived him, was his daughter, Fatimah, and his son-in-law, Ali, who was his cousin as well.

This small minority said, "We want the bloodline through Ali," whereas the majority said, "No, it [the succession] has to be through the disciples or companions who were with him from day one, because from day one, Ali was only eight years old. He was still a little boy."

Well, the majority won. Ali got pushed off three times. Not until three successors after Muhammad was he a successor. Up until then, Islam was united. But after Ali, the war between the majority and the minority started.

Basically, the majority, who are the Sunni, eliminated the lineage of their own prophet. It continued up until the Twelfth Imam—you've heard that term, *Imam* or *Mahdi*—and they tried to assassinate him. He went to a cellar in Iraq, or Ramadi. In that location, he disappeared.

That's why, to this day, the Shia commemorate the death of every person of the lineage of Ali, or the lineage of Muhammad, during the month of Ashura. This is observed with ten days of mourning.

They believe Al-Mahdi is still alive, and they teach that at the end of time, he will appear. The Qur'an says that 'Îsa, or Jesus, will also appear at the end of time, but he will be subservient to Al-Mahdi, the Twelfth Imam. This Twelfth Imam will not show up until there is a global holocaust. That's why the Iranians, Ahmadinejad and other leaders in Iran, want to have nuclear weapons. They want a global nuclear war so they can usher in the time for Al-Mahdi to come.

James: They believe they can instigate the end times by creating this holocaust?

Elijah: Right.

James: In Baghdad—

Elijah: Let's go back to the differences again. That's how it all started. The Sunni are the majority, and they have the ulama, or scholars, and the fatwa, and those are mainly centered in Al-Azhar University in Cairo. Out of that came the Muslim Brotherhood, and from the Muslim Brotherhood came other different organizations.

The Shia are mainly concentrated in Iran, and the majority of Muslims in Iraq are Sunni. You've got southern Lebanon, and Hezbollah, which are usually Shia. You've got the Houthis in Yemen. You've got some Shia pockets in Pakistan, Afghanistan, and maybe Armenia, and some other places such as Bahrain. That's why Saudi Arabia annexed Bahrain—because the Arab spring was coming from there. They annexed it because the emir, the prince of Bahrain, said, "We need your help. We need intervention to keep our sovereignty."

James: About the Twelver: Is that usually a different name or title?

Elijah: Yes, the Twelver is the Twelfth Imam. Also, within both the Shia and the Sunni there are multiple sects. Ultimately, their doctrine, the Hadith of the Shia, is really of Ali—what he said, what he did, and of course what Muhammad said and did too. The Hadith of the Sunni is comprised of what Muhammad said, and usually [reliable Hadith such as] al-Bukhārī, and so on.

James: Let me ask you: Is this enmity still ongoing to this day?

Elijah: Absolutely.

James: You were a minority, then, in Baghdad, in Iraq.

Elijah: Yes.

James: How did that affect you?

Elijah: We always felt inferior to the rest of the Muslims. Saddam Hussein was a Sunni, but he was a secular Muslim. He did not care about Shia, Sunni, or Christians. He eliminated the communists because he was a socialist dictator, and he hated communism.

Also, he put down the Muslim Brotherhood. He killed them all. The Muslim Brotherhood could not survive there. He also put down and eliminated a political party called the *Dawa*.

Saddam Hussein said, "I am the emperor. Don't you challenge me. If you want to live in peace, keep your mouth shut." That's what he told the Christians. By the way, he trusted the Christians more than the Muslims. But the Christians still could not do what they wanted. When I was in Iraq, I did not even know that they existed. Not until I came to the United States and met some evangelical Iraqis who had escaped did I know there are Christians in Iraq. They had been imprisoned by Saddam.

The visible church—the Catholics, Armenians, Caledonians, and others, the Orthodox—Hussein told them, "Look, you can exist. I'll give you protection. But keep your gospel, your Christianity, in the church." They did, unfortunately. He kept the peace by force. It was a police state. Once he was gone, everything unraveled.

The Shia hate the Sunni. They have never forgotten what the Sunni did long ago to Ali and his descendants. That's why every year they observe with mourning. My father used to observe this. Toward the end of the ten days, the Shia would cook and give the food to the poor, and do other things like that.

You can look it up online. Some of these Shia—in London, for example—they beat themselves with chains and swords. They commemorate the deaths of those killed by the Sunni. The theology between the two is a bit different, but there are common denominators. One common denominator is Allah. Another is that Muhammad is a prophet. Another is that Islam is superior to any other religion. They differ more on the little things, just like other groups.

James: While you were growing up Shia, did you know about Jesus or hear about Him? Anything at all?

Elijah: I heard that He was a prophet of Allah, just like any other prophet. All the names in the Bible—they're all prophets. They say that Islam did not start with Muhammad; it started with Adam, because Islam is the religion of Allah. Adam was a prophet, and every person in the Old Testament was a prophet. And ʿĪsa, or Jesus, was also a prophet.

James: Your total knowledge of Jesus was that you knew His name, and that He was one of the prophets—

Elijah: He was one of the prophets. He was born of the virgin Mary, or Maryam, according to the Qur'an. He did miracles. He created a bird out of a clay, which comes from the Apocrypha.

James: This is something you read in the Qur'an, or you were taught in—

Elijah: We were taught in school, and it's in the Hadith. It's well known among Muslims—both the Shia as well as the Sunni. Jesus raised the dead. He healed the sick. But He did not do it in His own power or authority. He was only a prophet, a messenger. Everything He did was done through Him by Allah.

James: Did it ever cross your mind that Jesus could be God?

Elijah: No, because that's the ultimate blasphemy. There are six doctrines in Islam. You have the five pillars of Islam. Those comprise the practice of Islam. The six doctrines are nonnegotiable. First is Allah, who is one, and not triune.

James: Tawhid.

Elijah: Yes, tawhid. To say Jesus, or 'Îsa, is God is blasphemy. That's an unforgivable sin. The second doctrine has to do with angels. The third doctrine is about the end time, or judgment day. Then they have predestination, and the holy books, or the Torah, the Zabur, which is the Psalms and the Gospels.

James: Just an aside: When Muslims say they believe the gospel, which gospel is it that they believe?

Elijah: Thank you very much for asking that. They say all the Gospel of 'Îsa.

James: The Gospel of Jesus?

Elijah: Right. Allah inspired 'Îsa to give the Gospel.

James: Would that be Matthew, Mark, Luke, and John?

Elijah: No, because those books are corrupt, as far as they're concerned. The Islamic version of Jesus's arrest and "crucifixion" is different. In the Bible, when the soldiers came to arrest Jesus, He stood up and said, "Who do you seek?" The soldiers said, "Jesus of Nazareth." Jesus said, "I am." When they heard, "I am," they fell to the ground.

But the Jesus of the Qur'an was a coward. He escaped, went to a cave, and Allah raptured Him. Allah took Jesus like he took Elijah [the prophet in 2 Kings 2].

One of the disciples who followed after 'Îsa, Allah changed his [appearance and] features so that he looked like 'Îsa. Now, some believe the identity of that [disciple] whose features were changed is Judas Iscariot, because he betrayed his master. What happened to this Gospel, the Injil? Allah took it with 'Îsa. I ask Muslims, "What's the point of sending the Gospel, of sending the prophet 'Îsa, only to take that message back with Him? Isn't that message supposed to be for all mankind?" They say no.

The Muslim Jesus is not the same Jesus as the Christian one. I get upset when I hear evangelical Christians, those who are supposed to have the right knowledge—whether it be professors or missionaries or pastors—say it's the same Jesus. That's blasphemy, as far as I'm concerned, because you are comparing a fictitious character created by Muhammad with the true, living Son of God.

James: Do you think Muhammad may have heard stories on the caravan routes and maybe—?

Elijah: I'm glad you asked that, because Muhammad's understanding of Judaism and Christianity is all hearsay. Muslims brag that he was illiterate; he could not read. Also, during his lifetime, the Bible was not available in Arabic—so he had no access to the gospel. Where did he get his information from? The practices of Jewish people? The washing, the prayer (five times instead of three times), a lot of the dietary laws—where did he get all that from? Very likely, the caravan journeys.

James: Do you think he confused the story of the virgin Mary with that of Mariam, the sister of—?

Elijah: Absolutely, because you have to understand, he—

James: —the sister of Aaron and Moses.

Elijah: You have to look at the context of where Muhammad lived.

There were heretic Jews, heretic Christians, and during that period of time, there were the Nestorians.[2] Muhammad rejected the Trinity. The question is, which Trinity? He rejected God the Father, Jesus the Son, Mary the mother. I reject that Trinity, and so do you.

Muslims never look beyond that because they trust that their prophet knew what he was talking about. But he was a victim of his own ignorance about what the Bible truly says, and what Jesus truly said. When Muhammad had his first encounter with this spirit—he called it *wahy*—He did not even know the name of the angel. Not until he went to Medina twelve years later did he hear about this guy named Gabriel. "That must be him," Muhammad said.

Look at how Scripture describes people's encounters with an angel. It's scary to meet an angel. That's why, in Scripture, when angels meet people, the first words out of their mouths are "Fear not," or "Do not be afraid."

That did not happen with Muhammad. He was scared out of his mind. To save time, I'm not going to go into the conversation between him and the angel, but he went home, got into his bed, and begged his heretic Christian wife Khadijah, "Cover me; cover me."[3] [Implying that he may have been] touched by a demon.

But if Muhammad was truly a prophet of the almighty God, why did he react differently than Moses [Exodus 3]?

James: That's all in the Hadith?

Elijah: That's in the Hadith, yes. How did Muhammad realize he was a prophet? His wife proved to him that he was a prophet. How? She said, "Is that spirit in the room?" He said, "Yes." He was still shaken. She said, "Let's see whether this spirit or angel is from Allah." She took off her shirt, then asked, "Is he still there?" Muhammad said, "Yes." Then she took off her clothes and became naked. "Is he still there?" she asked. He said, "No, he disappeared." "See?" she said. "He's a holy angel. You're from Allah."

James: Can you tell us more about Nestorian Christianity? Why were the Nestorians considered heretical, and not a part of mainstream Christianity?

Elijah: The Nestorians believed in a false Trinity. They did not believe that Jesus was God. They believed He was a prophet, a Savior, but not fully man, fully God.

James: Maybe this is where Muhammad got the idea that Jesus is not the Savior.

The Shia, like the Sunni and other Muslims, believe that Jesus was born of a virgin.

Elijah: Right.

James: Is that in the Qur'an?

Elijah: Yes. But they say Jesus was not born of the Holy Spirit. That's why, when I talk with a Muslim, I don't start by talking about Jesus. If you ask a Muslim, "Do you believe Jesus was born of a virgin?" he will say, "Yes, but that happened by the power of Allah." They reason that in the same way that Allah was able to create Adam from dust, he was able to create 'Īsa from a virgin.

James: While they would say, "Jesus is Son of Maryam or the son of Mary," they would never say, "Jesus is the Son of God."

Elijah: No, because that goes against doctrine number one, which is tawhid. Allah is one.

James: I'm going to ask you later about how you came to Christ. Before you became a believer, when was the first time you heard someone call Jesus the Son of God?

Elijah: In Iraq, from the Christians.

James: From the Christians in Iraq?

Elijah: Sure.

James: What was your feeling when you heard that term?

Elijah: Upset. Kafir, infidels. How could they say that? Allah is one.

James: Did you also sense the idea that they were implying there was some kind of sexual relationship behind this?

Elijah: No.

James: That did not cause confusion for you?

Elijah: No.

James: If Jesus was born of a virgin, that automatically says there was nothing sexual.

Elijah: Right, but unfortunately, we're talking about translators and others who make it out to be sexual. They say, "Well, the Muslims look at it as sexual." That's reading into it. No Muslim I have witnessed to has talked about this in sexual terms.

Going back to when I first heard more about Jesus, the first seed that God planted in my life was planted at the elementary school I went to in Iraq. This gives you an idea of how God works in wonderful and miraculous ways. The elementary school was a private school at the time, and it was Christian.

James: You went to a Christian school?

Elijah: Yes, and Muslims loved the education there because it was a quality education. They were willing to pay for it. In Lebanon, the best schools are Baptist or evangelical schools. In Jordan, one of the best schools has a waiting list to get in. It starts from kindergarten and goes all the way to high school. It was started by Baptists.

James: The Muslim parents don't like the madrasas [a school in which Islamic sciences or Quranic scriptures and ideologies are studied]?

Elijah: Right, because they want their kids to get a quality education. Same thing in Iraq. But at the school I went to—I don't know if it still exists—I had Christian friends and Muslim friends. I always wanted to be with the Christians, because I felt a peace with them. With my Muslim friends, including my family members, it was like we were at war, constantly battling each other and arguing with each other.

These Christian people, they were peaceful. I wanted to be with them. I believe that was the first seed God planted. When I was with my Christian friends, I heard the name *Yeshua*, which is Jesus. I was confused. I said, "Wait a minute—Yeshua? What is that? A title? Is that the same as 'Îsa? They said, "No, he is not the same. Yeshua, He is the Son of God."

But then they said, "'Îsa al-Masih" ["Jesus the Messiah"]. I didn't understand. I asked Muslims, "Could you please define what *al-Masih* means?" They didn't know. They thought maybe that was His title. Again, that's why when I witness to Muslims, I do not start with Jesus. Instead, I start on the fundamentals, and the number one obstacle is the Trinity, which I have to explain.

James: You've already touched on this a little.

Elijah: We could touch on it again if you want me to [laughs].

James: Let's talk about Jesus on the cross. For the Christian, this is the center of their faith. You have a gospel that is about the death, burial, and resurrection of Christ, and His death on the cross. There's no Christianity without the cross. There's no gospel without it. No Muslim that you know of—

Elijah: Believes in the cross. That—

James: No Shia—

Elijah: Shia or Sunni. Throughout the whole Muslim world, the Jesus of the Qur'an never died on the cross. He did not even reach the cross. He went to a cave and was raptured. They believe 'Īsa is still alive and that He will come back again.

James: He never died?

Elijah: Never died.

James: No Muslim then, no Shia, no Sunni, is going to believe that Jesus is the Savior of the world.

Elijah: Correct.

James: Let me ask you: In Islam, who is the savior?

Elijah: There is no savior. In Islam, salvation is works-based.

James: As a Muslim, as a Shia, how were you told to become saved?

Elijah: There is no such thing as becoming saved. The whole idea of Islam, whether you are Shia or Sunni, is that you do the five pillars of Islam. You follow the teachings and be obedient, and you do all the things a pious Muslim does. When you die, you are at the mercy of Allah on the Day of Judgment. He will weigh the good works versus the bad works.

James: Put your good deeds on one side, and your bad deeds on the other.

Elijah: Right. Now, even if I did the best I could, even if I did good works, I still have bad deeds on my record. Muhammad said every Muslim has to go through hell first to pay for his bad deeds. That's Islamic purgatory. People asked him, "Including you?" He said, "Including me." That contradicts the teaching that all Muslims are infallible, including Muhammad.

If Muhammad was infallible, why would he have to go through hell to pay for his sins before he could enter paradise? That's why one Muslim I spoke with said, "Yes, I believe in Allah's law, and I believe what Islam teaches. Yes, I might end up in hell, but ultimately, I'm going to paradise." The question is this: How long will he have to stay in hell? It all depends on how many bad works he performed. It's all works-based.

James: Are there any Muslims who have assurance that they are going to paradise?

Elijah: Yes—jihadists who die for the sake of Allah and for defending Allah. That's why the hijackers in 9/11 went to a strip bar the night before they crashed the planes. As far as they were concerned, "While I'm here in the physical world, I'm going to enjoy the physical pleasures, because tomorrow, the moment I hit that building, all of my sins are forgiven, I will immediately be in paradise, and I'm going to have seventy-two virgins." By the way, they're going to sleep with boys too—virgin boys. You compare paradise to heaven. Even paradise, it's a garden of orgies and drunkenness and so on.

James: Were you happy as a Muslim?

Elijah: Define *happiness*.

James: Content. Spiritually happy.

Elijah: No.

James: Did you feel like you had a connection with Allah?

Elijah: No. You feared Allah. When you say to a Muslim, "Do you have a personal relationship with Allah?" he will say that's blasphemy.

James: Because of shirk, you get back into the same problem that you—

Elijah: Let me explain to you the concept of Allah. Imagine this table is the universe. We, planet Earth, is right here; we're on planet Earth. Allah says, "Let there be light. Here's the universe. Here's the Qur'an. I'll see you on judgment day." There's no relationship. When we Christians say that God Himself sent His Word to come down to Earth, Muslims say that's blasphemy because God does not come down to Earth. This is degrading to Him. The incarnation is degrading to Him.

Muslims ask me this: "Are you saying that Allah comes down to Earth, gets hungry, goes to the bathroom, and then gets crucified? That's a weak Allah." I say, "You don't understand the love of God." I also tell them, "Your Allah is weak. He cannot do anything. My God can do anything He wants to do."

Here is how I explain the incarnation. I say, "Do you believe God is one?" They answer, "Yes." I tell them, "My Bible also says God is one. Do you believe the God of the Old Testament appeared to Moses in a burning bush?" They have to say yes because that's in the Qur'an. Muhammad heard the story, and the only thing Muhammad got right is the event itself. But the conversation between God and Moses, as recorded in the Qur'an, is totally different.

James: There was a burning bush?

Elijah: Right. I ask, "The event that happened at the burning bush—do you believe that?" They'll say, "Yes; it's in the Qur'an." That's when I point out, "So you agree that God came down to Earth to communicate to Moses from a burning bush. Who do you think you are to tell Him He cannot come down to Earth in the form of a man to die for you and for me?"

Immediately they say, "No, no, no, he can do that." I say, "Hold on. Allah is not your Allah. First you say he cannot come to Earth because it is degrading to him. Now you say he can come to Earth." I point out this contradiction to them.

The gospel is simple. What is it? I studied the life of Jesus and boom, it became clear to me. He did the practical things. He fed people. He ate with them. He prayed for them. He healed the sick. He did all of that. He always asked questions, and He answered questions with a question.

James: You never felt spiritually fulfilled and you never felt—

Elijah: No.

James: Did you ever pray…? Let me ask this another way: Do Muslims ever pray outside the obligatory daily prayers?

Elijah: Yes, they call those petitions.

James: Petitions.

Elijah: I remember my parents did this, and I tried to copy my parents. I did the same thing.

James: It's not a conversation, though. It's just a—

Elijah: It's being a beggar, it's being a slave to a master because that's the kind of relationship it is. Allah is similar to a master over a slave, not similar to a father over a son, like that in the Scriptures. After we finished our [obligatory] prayer, we petitioned about whatever was going on in our life. But we had no assurance that Allah had heard us or was going to answer our petitions.

James: Tell us about your transition into Christianity. Take us through that journey.

Elijah: My dad smuggled me out of the country because the Iran-Iraq war had just started. A lot of young men died from that war. I was a young teenager when it began—I was about thirteen or fourteen years old. He got me out of the country. It cost him almost $100,000 to smuggle me out, and I ended up in Europe. There, I went to school and learned English. Some of my friends were Catholics who didn't go to church, but they invited me to visit a church for Easter or Christmas, and I really liked the experience, even though I did not understand what it was all about.

One of the schools I attended in England had chapel every morning, and during that time they sang hymns. I did not sing along with them. Instead, I just read the words and thought, *I really like this, but I don't understand what it means.* I would listen to the headmaster teach about what he read from Scripture. Even though I did not understand what he was saying, in the back of my mind I was thinking, *I like this.* God kept planting seeds in me.

Then I had problems with the Iraqi embassy, and there were death threats on my life. So I came to the United States. I found myself all alone; I did not know anyone. I thought, *Allah must be punishing me.* I started praying five times a day and became a devout Muslim, because up until that time I was—

James: Muslim by name only?

Elijah: Yes. Up until that point, I was a Muslim by name only, like millions of other Muslims. Many are Muslims by identity. They know the basics. It's ingrained into them from the moment they are born.

James: Whispered in your ear.

Elijah: That's it. This time I'm an adult. I can speak and read English, no problem. I can think for myself. I have an engineering background, so I can do analytical thinking for myself. I was doing everything that Islam asked me to do. I became devout. I grew a beard; read the Qur'an, trying to understand it; read the Hadith, trying to understand it. You talk about confusion. I was begging Allah, "Please help me." I did not hear a thing.

My engineering-trained analytical mind thought, *Okay, there's a problem. Red flag.* I decided I would look at things from an equation point of view. In a mathematical equation, the left side has to equal the right side. You work the equation to find out the value of *x*. Here was the problem: Either God does not exist, or He does exist and I'm not talking to Him the right way.

I knew God existed because creation told me that. Thank God I did not buy into evolution. I exist, so if Allah created me, then the problem must be the way I was talking to him. However, I had tried to talk to him in the Islamic way, but it was not working. Was there any other way?

I was desperate, close to suicidal. I said, "What if Islam is not the way?" I got a piece of paper and I wrote down all the world religions. I started with Christianity, and I wanted to go through them using a process of elimination. If I can't find you here, God, I'm going to go to Judaism next. If not, then Mormonism, Jehovah's Witnesses, New Age, whatever it is. I had made a pact with God. "If I can't find You in this list, it's between You and me. I need You."

This is the beautiful thing about Scripture. It says that when you seek Him with all your heart, you will find Him [Jeremiah 29:13]. Thank God Christianity was on the top of the list. At the time, I knew nothing about Christianity. All I knew was that churches were buildings with a cross on a steeple. I knew nothing about denominations, knew nothing about Catholicism.

The nearest church to me was a Baptist church. I went to it. If it had been a Methodist church, I would have gone to it. If it had been a Catholic church, I would have gone to it. It did not make any difference to me. I was desperate. I needed God. If God was in the church, hopefully the people would tell me.

By the way, I made that decision right then and there. Everything I knew about Jesus from the Qur'an, I put it aside. I wanted to hear from Christians about who Jesus is, and who God is. I told God, "If it's not true, then I'm moving on."

James: Even before you made that transition to Christianity you could already sense there was a different God, a different Jesus? You knew that?

Elijah: I knew because they believed He's the Son of God, and we didn't. They said triune God, and we didn't. We said, "You have the wrong idea about who God is. You have the wrong idea about who Jesus is. We have 'Îsa. We know because the Qur'an is the final Scripture. Muhammad is the final prophet. How dare you say Allah is wrong."

James: Had your Christian friends told you, "We believe in the same Jesus, the same God?"

Elijah: Not in Iraq.

James: I know, but if they had, that could have hindered you from understanding the gospel.

Elijah: I would have said, "If we both have the same Jesus, why do you call Him the Son of God?" I probably would have started arguing and fighting with them. That's why I say Jesus is not a starting point [for discussion].

James: You went to a Baptist church.

Elijah: I went to a Baptist church. This is the beautiful thing: I have a lot of Christian friends who came from a Muslim background. Every Christian that I know from Muslim background, when I asked them how they came to know the Lord, they came in different ways. For me, it was analytical—seeking God by myself. Of course, not by myself; God put that desire in me. He drew me to seek Him.

The most important thing to me was the love Christians showed to me. The love of Christ, through the body of Christ, they showed it to me and did not even care where I came from.

When I walked into that church, everyone welcomed me and gave me hugs. This was at a desperate time in my life. Especially the old ladies, the grandmas—they gave me hugs. I had seen my mom at that time; I was thirteen years old. And I saw her only one more time after that, around 1990 or 1991. Other than that, it's like my family doesn't even know me.

When I sat down, the guy who helped me—an usher—said, "Are you sitting by yourself? Come sit with my family." In the back of my mind, I thought, *We don't do this in the mosque. He doesn't know me, yet he trusts me to sit with his wife and baby.* She said, "Come on, have a seat." Then they started singing.

Before they sang, one of the leaders, an older deacon, said, "Let's pray. Everyone stood up and closed their eyes and bowed their head. I thought, *We don't do this in the mosque.* I stood, closed my eyes, and bowed my head. I heard terminology I had never heard before. The deacon prayed, "Our Father in heaven." What? Who is our father in heaven?

I didn't know who He was, but I was sure they were going to tell me. Then the deacon said, "In Jesus's name I pray, amen." Wait a minute. *Amen* is a powerful word. It means "it is finished, it is done." It is irrevocable to say that after the name of Jesus. There was something special about the name of Jesus. When these people said amen after His name, I was all ears.

We sat down. Then someone said, "Let's stand." I thought, *These people like exercise.* The music started playing. The usher gave me a hymnal. What was I to do with this? He showed me the number on the page, and everyone started singing. I could read English, but I cannot sing, and I did not know the melody. But I was reading the text, and I thought, *I like this; this is wonderful.*

When the song finished, I closed the hymnal. I started watching the people. Some had their hands raised, with tears on their faces. Some had smiles on their faces, some of them were reading and nodding. When they sang, they did it with all their hearts. I thought, *Who are they singing to? Who are they talking to?*

Then the pastor got up and started preaching, and he said things that Muslims object to. He was teaching out of John chapter 3. By the way, he said, "Open your Bible and turn to John chapter 3." I had no Bible; I just sat there. The man next to me said, "Here is my Bible." He put it in my lap, but it was closed. I thanked him, then said, "Excuse me, who is John?" I was clueless. He said, "One of Jesus's apostles." I asked, "What's an apostle?" He said, "One of His disciples." I asked, "What's a disciple?"

He said, "Jesus was a teacher, and they were His students." Teacher, students—I got it! "How can I find this John guy?" He helped me. As I was reading, the typical Muslim objections to the Trinity started popping up in my mind. One of them, of course, was in response to the famous verse John 3:16, which at the time I did not know was famous. That was the first time I had heard about the verse or read it.

The impact hit me like a ton of bricks. Three things jumped out at me. One, God loved me unconditionally. Two, He had a Son. How was it I didn't know about that? The salvation He offered was a gift. Even if I worked for it, I couldn't earn it. The third one was even more powerful, and that was the assurance of salvation.

No one in Islam has that assurance, even if they do the five pillars of Islam and believe in the six doctrines. Even if they do everything that Islam asks them to do, including follow Sharia law, when they die, they have no assurance of salvation. None. Except, of course, jihadists who die as suicide bombers or while fighting for Allah. After that, I looked at the usher and said, "Excuse me. What can I do to become Christian?" You should have seen his face!

James: That one passage, John 3:16—

Elijah: Yes. He was explaining it.

James: And seeing the people's faces, that there was something real about all this.

Elijah: The whole package. Everything I saw—that they were worshipping and experiencing a relationship with their creator—I didn't have, and Islam did not offer. By that time, I knew there was a problem with Islam: Allah does not speak. I realized that if Allah was truly the creator, he should at least have said hello. If he spoke the universe into existence, why couldn't he speak to one of his creations? I knew right then, *God lives here.*

I asked the man, "What can I do to become Christian?" He said, "Well, you go up during the invitation." I said, "I'm not going up there by myself." He said, "I'll go with you." This man then took me all the way to the altar. I was confused. Had he heard what I had asked him? Maybe I asked him the wrong question. Actually, I had asked the right question, but at the same time, I had asked the wrong one.

I had asked the right question because I was desperate for God. And I had asked the wrong question because I was approaching Christianity by works, like a Muslim. What can I *do*? The man was showing me what to do. He did not understand my background or my belief system. When we got to the front, the preacher led me to Christ by prayer, right then and there. He baptized me that evening. For six years in that church, I thought I was saved, but in reality I wasn't.

James: You were just looking for another set of works to do—instead of doing shahada, you walked the aisle. Instead of doing salat, you prayed that one prayer. You were looking for a set of works to appease God.

Elijah: Right, I approached Christianity that way. I had made up my mind. I was going to be the best I could as a Christian. I became an usher. I drove the minivan and the bus, I was involved in outreach, I was doing everything. I was single, I had the time to do all this until I met my wife. For the first time in six years, I saw a born-again believer every day. Until I met her, I saw believers only once a week for an hour or two, and maybe on Wednesday night. But now I saw one every day because I was in love.

I thought, *She's got something I don't have. She has peace, contentment, and joy, and I don't.* I was working very hard at this, and every Sunday I was repenting for something. After six years of this, I still had no peace. When I got engaged, I was having this debate within myself. I got out the Qur'an, got out the Bible, and I compared them. I wondered if maybe I was still wrong.

James: That's six years after you walked down the aisle. Just to ask you a quick aside, do you feel that this is a problem only for Muslims who become Christians, or for anyone?

Elijah: Do you know what I tell people when I speak to them in American churches? I tell them that before I went to that Baptist church, I was a Muslim. If I had died, I would have gone to hell. When I went to that Baptist church, I became a Baptist Muslim. If I had died, I would have gone to hell.

I tell them, "Some of you sitting here are like Baptist Muslims, even though you're in a Bible church or a Pentecostal church or a Methodist church. A Baptist Muslim comes to church every Sunday, he tithes, he memorizes one or two prayers just in case he is called upon to pray: 'Hey would you please lead us in prayer?' He only reads verses that are easy to understand; he does not truly understand the message of Scripture. He memorizes what Jesus did, but he's still empty. He's doing all this as a Baptist Muslim."

James: Let me ask you this: Six years after the time you walked the aisle, you thought you were a Christian, but you were not—

Elijah: I wasn't.

James: —you saw in your wife something that you knew was genuine, and you knew you didn't have that as a Muslim or as a Baptist. At that point, did you understand the gospel?

Elijah: No, that's what the problem was. I wish they would simplify the gospel in American churches. Sometimes we complicate things because of our theological degrees. The gospel is simple. This idea of inviting people to come forward means the possibility of false confessions. They don't talk about repentance.

A person needs to make a 180-degree turn, and we need to make this clear. Thank God I did not die during those six years. It upsets me when I see pastors who are like a used car salesman. They ask people to come forward so they can brag, "We had two baptisms today." We're talking about the souls of men and women in our hands when we preach, so we had better get the gospel right.

James: How did you come to understand?

Elijah: Remember when I compared the Qur'an and the Bible to see which was true? I realized the Qur'an is not. And I opened the Bible and prayed, "God almighty, I know You are the God of this Bible. I know this is true. I know there's something wrong here. I'm going to read the Gospels, the Old Testament, and please show me from Your Word whether I'm born again. Assure me. If I'm not born again, convict me. I do not want to live like this."

Guess what? God convicted me about two months after that prayer. For the next four or five months, I was tormented by Satan not to make that decision. I was afraid and thought, *What will people think when they find out I hadn't been saved those six years?* That is a typical Middle Eastern mindset, and I did not realize it's also an American mindset. It's called pride. We worry about what other people will think.

James: Was there a particular passage of Scripture you were studying when this began to occur to you?

Elijah: There were a few of them. One of them was Ephesians chapter 1, where it talks about how we have been adopted in Christ Jesus, we have heaven and earth, and we are sealed with the Holy Spirit. I realized that if I were sealed, then I would have that peace. But I knew I didn't have that peace. Jesus said, "My peace I give to you, not as the world gives" [John 14:27]. If He had given me that peace, why was I feeling this way? Then I read through Romans, and all through the first five chapters, I felt conviction after conviction.

James: I remember when a clear understanding finally came to me one day. One night I would pray that God would forgive my sins and give me eternal life. But then the next night, I would make the same request again. It eventually occurred to me that I didn't have His forgiveness, or I wouldn't keep asking for it.

Elijah: Finally, in Ephesians, I read that we are saved by faith through grace, and not by works.

James: Ephesians 2:8-9.

Elijah: That's what I had been doing—salvation by works. What did "by faith" mean? I had to do some studying, and finally, I noticed that on Pentecost, when Peter was preaching, the people were cut to the heart and they asked, "What must we do to be saved?" He said, "Repent and believe and be baptized." Repentance? I looked that up in the dictionary. Oh, that's what I need to do! That's when I realized I was still lost.

The next four or five months, during our engagement, Satan used that against me. He put me in fear. "You're okay, you're saved," he said. That should have been a red flag for me. But I did not know where those thoughts were coming from. I was in torment because now I had a fiancée, and she thought I was saved.

Then I joined eighty other guys from our church to attend a Promise Keepers rally in the old stadium in Irving, Texas. There were 70,000 to 75,000 people there.

James: At Texas stadium.

Elijah: Yes. God was all over me. That took place October 27, 1995, on my birthday. I remember the Lord telling me, "I brought you to this country for a reason; let me in." I did not hear this audibly. But I could sense God saying, "When you stand before Me—not your pastor, not your fiancée, not your church—nobody will defend you except My begotten Son, who died naked in front of all of Jerusalem." All this time, I was a mess. I was sobbing.

I saw the other guys around me. I knew I had to follow God, not man. I got up and went to the pastor, who was two rows behind me. I grabbed him by the hand and said, "I need to talk to you." He took one look at my face and said, "Okay." We went to a concession stand; there was a lot of noise around us. I told him exactly what I'm telling you. He smiled. I said, "What are you smiling about? I'm a mess here."

He said, "I'm not laughing at you." Here I was, cut to the heart. I knew I was lost, but I didn't know what to do about it, and I didn't care what other people thought. The pastor said, "Were you at church last night, the last day of the revival?" I said, "No. I had to work late." He said, "I've been married twenty-five years, and I've been in the ministry twenty-four years. Last night, my wife finally got saved." I said, "What?"

He said, "I've seen it happen before. I've seen senior citizens walk down the aisle sobbing, people who have been at the church thirty, forty, fifty years." I said, "I have been doing this for six years." He said, "Don't get upset. Let me tell you something." I'll never forget what he said—I'm sure you've heard of the concept before. That was the first time I had heard of it.

He said, "The distance between heaven and hell is about eighteen inches, from the head to the heart." I said, "I'm thirty-two inches, I believe." He said, "Yes, you are. You're playing politics with God." I said, "Actually, I'm playing Russian roulette." He was still talking to me, and I ignored all the noise around us. I got down on my knees and cried out to God.

"Father, forgive me. I've sinned before you, I've sinned before man. I've blasphemed the name of Jesus all my life. Now I know He's my Savior. He died for me, He rose from the dead three days later. Come into my life and save me. I repent. Help me walk the Christian walk by Your Spirit; help me." It all hit me like a huge wave. The pastor reached down, lifted me up, and hugged me. He said, "Welcome to the family of God." He didn't even have to lead me and say, "Pray after me" because I had already prayed.

James: You just flowed, just you and God.

Elijah: Yes, that's it.

James: You and God.

Elijah: I went back to my seat. Did not know what to say to the others.

James: Elijah, do you still have contact with your Muslim family?

Elijah: Some of my sisters cut me off when they found out I was going to church during that period of six years. They disowned me until my mom needed financial help for a surgery. I did not have the money, so I borrowed it and sent it to them. I thought that might open the door to them.

In a Muslim family, when someone converts to Christianity, that person is disowned. He is no longer welcomed. I wanted to show them that I still loved them, still cared for them. They were still my family, but I wanted nothing to do with Islam. They tolerated me, but from a distance. If I were to go to Iraq, they would put a bullet in my head. My own father would have done that—that's what he told me at one point. As far as immediate family members—

James: You can't go back to Iraq.

Elijah: I can.

James: I mean safely.

Elijah: Not to them, no. In 2010, after thirty years of absence from Iraq, I went to northern Iraq for a pastors' conference, and that was an incredibly emotional trip. It was good to see these evangelicals who were not present when I lived in Iraq, and now they are there.

James: There's a healthy church in Iraq?

Elijah: They are being persecuted right now big time. I don't know what their status is going to be. I heard a Christian leader in the Middle East say, "The visible church sooner or later will leave the Middle East because we're visible. The ones who will carry the torch of Christ are the converts like you."

James: One final question for you. A lot of Christians here and around the world know Muslims as neighbors, friends, coworkers—everything from pharmacists to the community store clerk.

They are often fearful of trying to share their testimony or the gospel, or talking about the differences between Muslims and Christians. What advice would you have for Christians who want to talk to a Muslim about God?

Elijah: Any conversation has to start somewhere, and that start is to be a friend. You have to develop rapport. Why would someone open their heart and share about everything to a stranger? Be friendly. Invite them to lunch or dinner or have coffee with them.

James: Almost all evangelism is built on the back of a relationship.

Elijah: Right. You need to have a relationship. Here is a statistic I heard back in 1999, and it still haunts me to this day. I believe that with today's technology and media and the Internet, this is changing. But the statistic is that from the time a Muslim first hears the gospel to the time he accepts Christ, it can take six or seven years.

James: Is it hard for God to reach a Muslim with His gospel?

Elijah: Was it hard to reach a terrorist named Paul?

James: We will wrap up on that point. Thank you so much.

Chapter 18

Interview with Zemara Campbell, Former Sunni Muslim

Zemara Campbell is a former Sunni Muslim who was raised in Pakistan. In this interview, she shares how she was introduced to Bible study through friends she met in America. She began to doubt her Muslim faith and the teachings of the Qur'an and went on to discover that Jesus was more than a prophet of God. She later accepted Him as her Lord and Savior.

James: Zemara, can you tell me about your background as a Muslim?

Zemara: I was born and raised mostly in Peshawar, Pakistan. I grew up in a family of eight, with three brothers and two sisters. We were a typical Muslim family, not a dedicated one. When we still lived in Pakistan, my older sister and mom both wore hijabs. I was under ten, so I didn't have to wear a hijab unless I went to school. It was an Islamic school, and the hijab was part of the uniform. When I went to the grocery store I didn't have to wear a hijab, but at school, I did.

James: And you went to the mosque and—

Zemara: Back home, there was no mosque for women.

James: Oh.

Zemara: It was mainly for men. Of course, we were off on Fridays, and all the men headed to the mosque. It was a big deal. My dad encouraged my brothers to go. Sometimes they would skip, but the majority of the time, they went. But the women stayed home, cooking and waiting for the men to come back from the mosque. It was a big deal for the whole city.

James: Mm-hmm.

Zemara: I mean, you could tell that it was a holy day. It wasn't like the Sundays here, which are so quiet [laughs]. It wasn't like that at home.

James: Did you do the daily prayers?

Zemara: As I was growing up, I did. In fact, in Peshawar, I had to study the Qur'an. I had to memorize parts of it to be able to pray. My dad was not so strict as to say, "You have to do the five daily prayers." He would encourage us, and I did pray. But I didn't do the five daily prayers every day.

During the time I was going back and forth between the United States and Pakistan, before my conversion, I would not leave my house or apartment without praying the morning prayer. That was something I felt I had to do, or the rest of my day would not go well.

James: As a Muslim, you were taught about Jesus. What did you believe? What were you taught?

Zemara: You know, that's an interesting question because the emphasis was not so much on Jesus. It was not so much about 'Îsa. I knew who He was. I knew He was a prophet. I knew He was there, but He was not part of the big picture. Muhammad was, and they made sure that you knew about Muhammad and not so much about 'Îsa or Jesus. That was never brought up in our family.

It was just something like, "Oh, yeah, He's a prophet." I knew who most of the prophets were. We were always told that many of the prophets did miracles and all that, but the emphasis on Muhammad was so great that we didn't talk much about 'Îsa.

James: Were you ever told any of the stories about Jesus or His miracles? Did you know anything except that He happened to be one of the prophets?

Zemara: No, I did not. As a matter of fact, I came to learn a lot more about 'Îsa when I was studying the Qur'an and the Bible—more than I had ever known up to that point in my life.

James: Wow. So in your study of the Qur'an—and I am guessing this was during that time when you were looking at both the Qur'an and the Bible—did you see where it teaches that Jesus was born of a virgin?

Zemara: Yes.

James: Did you already know that?

Zemara: I did not. As I said, we barely talked about 'Îsa. Our focus was that Allah is one, and that you praise him and Muhammad. There wasn't much about Jesus.

James: Were you ever taught that Jesus is God, or that He definitely was not God?

Zemara: We were not taught that. We were told God has no son, no partners. He is the only almighty, and there is no partner for Him. That was pretty straightforward, and they made sure to engrave that thought in your mind. For someone to think that God has a son or a partner was blasphemy.

James: Let me ask you about this: One of the big differences between Islam and Christianity is how the crucifixion is presented in the Gospel accounts and the Qur'an. What does the Qur'an teach about Jesus on the cross?

Zemara: It wasn't until I was learning about the Bible and studying the Qur'an that I began to know about this. I was never told these things. So the difference was something new to me.

James: The Bible talks about Jesus rising from the dead. Was this something you knew about when you were a Muslim?

Zemara: It was so foreign to me that I couldn't wrap my mind around it. It took me months to try to figure out, *What do I take from that?* It was just so foreign.

James: As a Muslim, what kind of relationship did you feel you had with God or Allah? Did you feel close? Did you feel like God, or Allah, loved you and was personally involved in your life?

Zemara: I felt like I needed to make sure that He was happy with me.

James: Trying to please or remember—

Zemara: Right, trying to please Him. I would do that.

James: How would you do that as a Muslim? How would you try to please God, or Allah?

Zemara: By praying, respecting my parents, being good to other people, doing good deeds, and being a good woman and being submissive. But that was the outside of me. Inside of me I had a relationship with God. I would talk to Him. I would pray to Him. It wasn't like, "I did my morning prayer. I'm done now." He was involved in my life.

James: The morning prayers or the obligatory prayers—they're always the same, and always spoken in Arabic, right?

Zemara: Correct.

James: Okay. But in addition to that, you also prayed personal prayers to God.

Zemara: I will not define those as prayers because it was more of talking to God and not prayer. For example, in college, or in school, when I submitted a paper or my homework or my test, I would say a quick prayer, then submit it. I would say something like, "God, please help me to pass this. Help me to pass this exam." I guess what I said was more for me than it was talking to Him.

James: Is your language Urdu?

Zemara: No, my language is Dari. D-A-R-I. Which is very similar to Farsi.

James: Farsi?

Zemara: Yes. Comparing Dari and Farsi would be like comparing Mexico's Spanish to Spain's Spanish.

James: Right. So when you would read the Qur'an, would you try to read the Arabic, or would you have a translation with you?

Zemara: Back in Pakistan, the only translation you can get is Arabic.

James: Could you read the Qur'an then?

Zemara: I was, because of—

James: Because of the school you were being taught in?

Zemara: It was mainly because the alphabets were very similar, and we went to a Quranic school. Arabic was taught in the school that we went to. It was like an after-school program, and they would help us learn Arabic. It wasn't difficult to read because the alphabets are similar.

James: As a Muslim reading the Qur'an, did you believe that one day you would face a judgment day?

Zemara: Yes, absolutely.

James: Tell me about that.

Zemara: Absolutely. We were told about judgment day. We never knew when it will come, so we had to continue doing good deeds.

James: What will happen on the Day of Judgment?

Zemara: I don't remember specifically what will happen. I was told it was going to happen, and I knew that there is a hell and a heaven. I knew that there is a God. There is no way that you can live in Pakistan and not know there is a God.

James: There is a hell and a heaven?

Zemara: Right.

James: And it all comes down to the Day of Judgment?

Zemara: Yes. I was told that when you die, your spirit would go to God, and God would ask you questions. "Did you do this? Did you do that?" Or, "Did you steal?" And if you try to say no, your tongue will start speaking about what you really did. That was like a fear tactic. Nothing about a loving relationship.

James: Did you have any assurance that on the Day of Judgment you would be loved by God, or…?

Zemara: No, it wasn't that. We had to fear him. We had to obey him because he has the power to do anything that he wants.

James: Did you ever feel like you could say, "I have done enough. I have assurance now because I have done all the requirements, so I should be fine on the Day of Judgment"?

Zemara: There was no such thing as enough. I didn't know what enough was. You had to continue doing good deeds. There is no such thing as enough.

James: Were you taught, or does it teach in the Qur'an, that Jesus is the Messiah?

Zemara: I was surprised to read that in the Qur'an.

James: What would that mean to a Muslim who reads that? I know you're not a Muslim now, but to read that as a Muslim—would that have any significance to you?

Zemara: As a Muslim I didn't know what Messiah was. I learned about that when I was studying both the Qur'an and the Bible for a year and a half. When I learned about Messiah in the Qur'an, it seemed foreign. I said to myself, "It's in here; how can you avoid this?"

And it says in the Injil, in the Gospels, it says that He is the Messiah. And again, it's repeated in the Qur'an. *How does all this work?* I wondered.

James: These questions about the Messiah and about Jesus came up as you were reading both the Qur'an and the Bible?

Zemara: Right.

James: What caused you to get to that point in your spiritual journey? What made you interested in reading the Gospels and the Bible?

Zemara: I will try to keep my answer short [laughs]. I met my husband in the library. We met at the University of Texas, Dallas, library. At first, I thought he was a typical American. You know, just another guy who wants to flirt. That's how I saw him. We were flirting back and forth, but nothing happened yet. When we returned after spring break of 2014, that changed.

We would workout—he did his thing, and I did my thing. He said, "I like you very much." I told him, "I've heard that before." He said, "I care about you." I responded, "Okay, that's great." Then he said, "I want you to be in heaven with me." I said, "That's new. I've never heard of that before." I thought, *He wants me to be in heaven with him. That's something forever. How could that happen?*

What he said got me thinking. Then he said, "Would you be willing to look into the Bible with me?" I took a minute to think about that. I thought, *Oh my. I don't know much about the Bible. How can I study it with him? Besides, the Qur'an is right. It doesn't matter what the Bible says. The Qur'an is the word of God. How can it be wrong?*

James: Before that day, how much of the Bible had you read?

Zemara: None.

James: None?

Zemara: None.

James: Was that unique for you? Or would you say most Muslims have never read one of the books of the Bible?

Zemara: I would be surprised if someone from a typical Muslim family had read any of the Bible. In Islam, we are told by our teachers and elders, "This is what you believe." I would be surprised to know that a Muslim had read the Bible, or the Zebur, or the Torah. I would also be surprised if most Muslims actually understand what they are reading in the Qur'an.

James: Are you saying that not only are Muslims not familiar with the stories of the Bible or the life of Jesus in the Gospels, but they also don't understand the Qur'an very much?

Zemara: That is correct. They are reading, but they don't understand what they are reading.

James: You might understand three or four words, or a few words?

Zemara: Yes. I don't know if they truly understand the whole message. I mean, it's—

James: Where does their theology and belief system come from? Is it from the Imams and the spiritual leaders, or from your family?

Zemara: From parents.

James: From parents?

Zemara: From parents. It's kind of like word of mouth. My parents got it from their parents. Their parents got it from their parents. It is passed along through the generations. They don't take their time to examine it.

James: Going back to this guy Wes…

Zemara: Yeah [laughs].

James: You were talking with him.

Zemara: Yes.

James: He was saying, "Why don't you read the Bible?" Were you a little hesitant?

Zemara: Oh yes. I was hesitant to pick up the Bible. I thought, *I shouldn't go close to it.* There were some people—they were Persians—who came from a church and talked with my dad. They gave him a copy of the Bible. But my dad placed that copy in his closet, and I would not go look at it.

James: Hmm.

Zemara: But when I was looking into the Qur'an and I wanted to look at the Bible, I went to his closet and got it. The Bible was not supposed to be in there, even though it is one of the four books we say we believe in.

James: Because the Qur'an does talk about the Bible, the Injil, the Gospels, and also the prophets of the Old Testament, right?

Zemara: When I started reading the Qur'an, I wondered, *How can you even understand this?* It is so hard to understand. It's like you need to be a scholar.

James: What about the Bible? Where did you and Wes start? Did you start in Genesis on page one, or did you—

Zemara: That's an interesting question, because we started in the Gospels, and we got into arguments. We broke up several times, and he got to the point where he became so emotional he said, "I cannot take this anymore. Just leave [laughs]." Because my mindset was to defend the Qur'an. I believed the Qur'an had to be right.

James: As you were reading the Gospels, what were some of the teachings that you resisted as a Muslim?

Zemara: Let me give you some background history as I answer that. We had so many arguments, he said, "I cannot stand to do this with you anymore." This was emotional for me as well because at first I was hesitant to read the Bible. But the more I studied the Bible with Wes's dad, the more comfortable I became with it.

One of the things that stood out to me was the sponge that the Roman soldiers offered to Jesus when He was on the cross. He declined it. I wondered, *Why would You decline it? Take it. You'll be in less pain.*

James: Did you ever find the answer to that question?

Zemara: Oh, yes.

James: I want you to share that with us.

Zemara: It was because Jesus wanted to go through that pain for all of us. He wanted to. He was willing to; He was wanting to give His life for our sins. He knew He didn't have to go through all that.

James: This was not an accident.

Zemara: Absolutely not.

James: Yes.

Zemara: No, He knew what would happen—He knew it from the beginning.

James: At what point in going through the Bible or the Gospels did you get the sense these things might be true?

Zemara: I started studying the Bible about April or May 2014. I was always defending the Qur'an until October 2014. I did that for six straight months. During that time, I was not sincere about searching for the truth. I believed the Qur'an was right. That's what I had been taught. It was in October 2014 that something clicked inside me, and I wanted to dedicate thirty minutes of my day looking into religion and faith in general. Also, I knew that Wes was reading a book called *Seeking Allah, Finding Jesus*.

James: Yes, by Nabeel Qureshi.

Zemara: Written by Nabeel Qureshi. I knew what Wes was reading; he told me about the author. I did a Google search, and I looked up one of Nabeel's videos. I realized we had something in common—he was from Pakistan, which is where I was born.

I figured he should know a lot. So I listened to his thirty-minute video. It was very interesting. He started with verses from the Qur'an. He started by speaking in Arabic, and I felt bad for the audience. I was like, "Good luck trying to understand that" [laughs]. Then he explained what he had said. As I listened, he addressed one of the questions I had thought about: If God can do anything, why can He not come to Earth? That's what I truly believed. I believed God can do anything He wants, no matter what.

James: Now that idea of God coming to Earth is not compatible with Islam, right?

Zemara: No, because—what's the other word for clean?—He's so sinless. He's so precious. He's so…Why would He want to come to Earth?

James: But what you were beginning to see is that nothing is impossible for God.

Zemara: Absolutely. I said, "If I believe that, then to say He wouldn't come to Earth means I am contradicting myself. If God can do anything He wants, why can He not come to Earth?" After all, in the next second, He can destroy this earth if He wants to.

James: In the Bible, you're reading about Jesus and you're learning that God loves His creation and loves human beings. Did you sense in the Qur'an that Allah, the God of Islam, is a God of love and grace?

Zemara: No. Allah is more a God of fear. It was more like, "Do this, or something will happen to you." There was so much fear that there was no such thing as love. It was different. The love from God in the Bible was warm to me. When I discovered this, I thought, *What is this? God cannot love; He is the creator. He's the King of kings. He has to be strict about what should happen.*

James: He has to be separate from creation.

Zemara: Correct.

James: He can't entangle Himself in any way with a partnership or becoming at all associated with the creation, right?

Zemara: Yes.

James: Which means us.

Zemara: It's interesting that you say that because when Wes's dad and I started looking at Genesis, everything changed for me. I said, "I know about this. I know about the creation. Yes, God did this." It's all in the Bible—that Earth was created in seven days, and so on. It was so amazing to know I could read about how God had created Earth. And that God was so involved with Adam and Eve. I learned about all that. Some of these details were in the Qur'an.

James: So you were feeling like there was some common ground? And that there was a ring of truth to what the Bible said?

Zemara: Right.

James: But the big breakthrough for you, if I understand correctly, was coming to the realization that if God is God, then He can do anything He wants, including come to Earth.

Zemara: Correct. It was in October of 2014 when I took the Bible more seriously. I said, "I'm questioning Islam, and that's not good" [laughs]. It wasn't good because I did not have peace in my heart.

James: Mm-hmm.

Zemara: I don't consider myself like a typical teenager who grows up in an American family or in any other family. My life was a little different. As a teenager, I looked up to the prophets and learned what they did so I could make my relationship with Allah stronger.

As I said earlier, during middle school and high school, my older sister and I would not leave the house without doing our morning prayer. We did this even when we were late to the bus. Sometimes we had to run to the bus because we had taken time to pray.

This wasn't something I did because it was passed down from my parents. I believed it. I practiced it. I did not practice it to the extent of a radical or a very strict Muslim family. I was trying to have a relationship with God and be closer to Him.

James: So you came to a place where you were honest with yourself. You were studying the Bible, and you were questioning Islam.

Zemara: Right.

James: And Islam wasn't looking good?

Zemara: Yes.

James: How did you resolve that? How did you make that transition from Islam to Christianity?

Zemara: I looked at the Bible differently. Wes's dad, who would go on to become my father-in-law, asked sincere questions. I would return home, and I was not at peace.

Wes's dad and I had Bible studies every single week for two hours. We would study, and then I would go back home and pray about what I was learning.

James: Let me ask you this: Did you dread those meetings with Wes's dad, or did you look forward to what you were going to learn next?

Zemara: It was like that. I found myself saying, "What's going to be next? I cannot defend Islam anymore."

Wes was looking into these things as well, even though we were not studying together. He was studying the Qur'an a lot more than I was.

James: So he was still involved in this process?

Zemara: Absolutely. Even though we were not studying together, he was doing his own research about Islam. He even told me something about the Qur'an that I never knew.

James: What was that?

Zemara: It was about chapter 4:32, about verses 32 to 35. It's about how a husband can hit his wife. That was not the God that I knew.

James: You didn't see this happen with any Muslim families in—

Zemara: You mean hitting their wife?

James: Right.

Zemara: Yes.

James: You did see that?

Zemara: Yes.

James: So the surprise to you was that the Qur'an endorsed it.

Zemara: The Qur'an says it.

James: Yes.

Zemara: And I knew it was practiced. When I saw that, I started crying.

James: Mm-hmm.

Zemara: I thought, *This was what my mom had to go through.*

James: Your mom?

Zemara: Yeah, my mom. She was…I can only say so much because it's—

James: Sure.

Zemara: But yes, the women that I knew—they were definitely beaten by their husbands.

James: Was that passage the final straw for Islam or for the Qur'an?

Zemara: The passage reminded me of the God that I did not know.

James: Wow.

Zemara: But the strongest point for me was that if God can do anything, He can come to Earth.

James: Which would mean He loves you.

Zemara: That's right. Which changed the world for me.

James: What was the day or the time? Was it in October? When and how did you come to say, "I don't believe the Qur'an anymore; now I believe Christianity and Jesus"?

Zemara: That was in December 2014. I did not believe in the Qur'an anymore. I knew it was not for me. There were so many things that I did not believe anymore. To be a Muslim, you have to believe the whole Qur'an. I had trouble with what it said about hitting a wife. It says if your wife did not listen, you advise her first. If she still doesn't listen, then you do not sleep with her. And if she still doesn't listen, you can hit her.

James: Mm-hmm.

Zemara: That's what was in my mind.

James: As you were losing faith in the Qur'an and learning things you did not know about Islam, was that being replaced at the same time with more faith in the Bible and in the Christianity?

Zemara: It was more faith toward God.

James: In God?

Zemara: In God. I said, "This is not the God that I know. He could not be this unloving."

James: At what point did you say, "I need to put my faith and hope in Jesus and not the Qur'an"?

Zemara: There was a lot of evidence in the Bible that I tried to ignore, but I couldn't do it anymore.

James: You could not.

Zemara: I could not. There were verses mentioned in the Gospels that were backed up in the Torah or in the Psalms. There was so much evidence that—

James: You had multiple testimonies from multiple sources.

Zemara: Correct. And the four books—Matthew, Mark, Luke, and John—how could they all be the same? They came from four different people. How could they all deliver the same message?

James: Mm-hmm.

Zemara: There was so much evidence I could not ignore it anymore.

James: When you became a Christian, did you tell your family? Do they know about this?

Zemara: Yes, they do. They know about it. Back in December 2014, I knew I was questioning Islam so much that I could not consider myself a Muslim anymore. I knew that I believed in God.

James: Atheism was never an option?

Zemara: No. I believe there is a God. There's no way that all of this around us can happen without God. I'm talking about everything—the moon, the sun, water—all of this could not have happened without God. The galaxy, the universe, how did they come about? They had to have come from someone bigger than us.

James: Mm-hmm.

Zemara: Atheism, or saying, "God does not exist," was not an option for me.

James: Mm-hmm.

Zemara: God *does* exist. Where is He, or what is He?

James: Did your family suspect that you might be a Christian?

Zemara: Back when ISIS crucified about a dozen different men or chopped off their heads, I had a conversation with my dad about it. I would back up my statements with the Bible. We were at home alone, and I could say only so much because I was afraid of his response. His last comment to me was, "If you ever believe in the Bible, you are no longer my daughter."

That happened before my marriage. As a daughter, of course my heart was hurt. I said, "I'm your daughter, and you just told me that?" I was thankful that he did not see my emotions because right after he said it, my mom walked into the room, and the conversation ended there. I don't know if that left any suspicions in my dad's mind.

James: But maybe a seed was planted.

Zemara: Yes. I can absolutely say that because when my husband and I were engaged, there were times where my dad would get angry with me and he would start saying bad stuff about Jesus. I cannot repeat what he said because he used bad words about Jesus. I was surprised and wondered, *Why are you cursing Jesus?*

James: Mm-hmm.

Zemara: I could not say anything in response because our wedding was getting close. I needed things to go well because I needed to get out of the house. I knew that with my dad's anger, it would not be a good idea for him to find out that I was a Christian while I was still living in the house. So I did not tell him about my conversion until after our marriage.

James: In that part of the world, is there such a thing as honor killing?

Zemara: Oh, yes.

James: Describe what that is, and why you could have been physically at risk.

Zemara: I cannot describe what it is because I have not personally seen an honor killing. But I can tell you this was on my mind. The story I'm about to share has nothing to do with Christianity. Several years ago, an Afghan family in Canada found out that their three daughters were dating others or doing things that were out of the norm for Muslim culture.
The brother killed his three sisters. That was because they had boyfriends. When the family found out what was going on, he killed the three girls.

James: So for some Muslims—not all—if a close family member, a sister or a wife, violates important beliefs and doctrines of Islam, the honorable thing to do is to kill them?

Zemara: You can do that if you're truly radical, if you truly believe that is what Islam teaches. But some families won't talk to the person anymore. They just exclude that person from the family.

James: Shunned.

Zemara: And from the community.

James: The incident with your dad happened several years ago. Are things any better now? Or are they about the same?

Zemara: No. I was recently reminded of him while listening to a song that says, "I will be there for you no matter what." My dad once said to me, "No matter what decision you make, I will always be there for you." Of course, he said that way before I started looking into Christianity.

That was a long time ago, and he was wrong, because he hasn't spoken to me or touched me for over a year and a half.

James: Do you think that reflects in some way the conditional acceptance of Allah, the God of Islam?

Zemara: Yeah, [my dad] wants to make sure to please his God. In his mind, he's doing the right thing. That's what the culture and Islam tell him to do. I am not surprised by the fact he hasn't talked to me for a year and a half. I told him about my Christianity in April 2016. I expected worse, and I continue to pray for us to be safe.

James: Based on your experiences during your journey from Islam to Jesus, what advice would you give to a Christian who knows a Muslim or has a Muslim friend? What could they do to help their friend to make a similar journey?

Zemara: I would say to establish a relationship with that person first. You might know a lot about Islam, and it's possible that person might not. Building a relationship will carry you a long way, rather than jumping on them and saying, "Muhammad did this, or Muhammad killed so many people, or he had so many wives, or he married, as some people say, a nine-year-old girl, or a thirteen-year-old girl." Stick to the Bible and stick to love, and tell that person how much you care and how much you want to see him or her in heaven.

James: Which was what Wes told you?

Zemara: Right.

James: And you remember that as if it happened yesterday, right?

Zemara: Absolutely [laughter].

James: As for a relationship—you're saying that you have to win the opportunity to be able to have those kinds of discussions, and you can't just jump into criticisms—

Zemara: Yeah.

James: —or attacks.

Zemara: Yeah. What's the point of bringing up something that's not worth spending your time on? Spend your time on what's important, which is the gospel.

James: And you said from your own experience that getting into the Bible, getting into the Gospels, you would recommend that a Christian invite a Muslim neighbor or friend to sit down to do Bible study together?

Zemara: Absolutely, and start in a place where you have a common ground, such as the book of Genesis.

James: Okay.

Zemara: I would think that a majority of Muslims know a little bit about Genesis, about how the world was created. One of the things that definitely helped me was when God said, "Let us make man"—and I'm paraphrasing this—"in our own image" [Genesis 1:26]. Who is "us"? God the Father, the Son, and the Holy Spirit.

James: Now you hinted at this a little bit, but we can't leave this story dangling out here—

Zemara: [laughs].

James: It never worked out with you and Wes, right?

Zemara: It did, because we're married now [laughs].

James: You married Wes. How long have you been married?

Zemara: We've been married since January 2016.

James: Congratulations on that—

Zemara: Thank you.

James: —and on a great testimony and story of the grace of God, and how anyone, regardless of their background, is not beyond a touch from the hand of God and the grace of our Lord Jesus Christ. Thanks so much for sharing.

Zemara: You're welcome. Thank you for having me.

God's Love Is Indescribable—
the Turning Point in My Life!

Zemara Campbell

Please allow me a final word to thank my Lord Jesus Christ and my new family that He used to reach me with His gospel of grace.

October 2014 through February 2015 was a different time in my life. I was myself, but lost within myself. Not to mention the Bible study that I had been doing with Wes's father (now my father-in-law) as early as April 2014 (I began the Bible study and religion discussions with Wes first). There was rarely a night that Wes and I would hang out without speaking about God's Word, the Bible, and the Qur'an.

I have thought about this so much that it was constantly in the back of my mind.

One night, I came home from work feeling exhausted. This was sometime in January or February. I knew I did not consider myself a Muslim anymore, and there were too many evidences from the Bible that I could not avoid. I did my nightly routines and got ready to go to bed.

Before going to bed, I usually like to talk to God about different things that are going on in my life, but this night felt different. My mind was full of thoughts and I was wearily active, so I closed my eyes and started by saying, "God, forgive me because I cannot accept

You for who You are." As soon as I said this statement, a pleasant person's face appeared right in front of me. The face of Jesus was right in front of me. I couldn't deny it. I knew from my heart that it was Him. Immediately, I said to God, "I will follow you no matter what it takes, even in spite of my parents." I accepted the truth within me.

I couldn't share this great news with Wes—not yet. After recognizing the greatness of our God, Jesus Christ, I couldn't share this happiness with the person who would be extremely thrilled to hear this wonderful news because I knew the cost, and because I loved my parents very much. On one hand, a heavy weight was lifted off of my shoulders. On the other hand, there was a high chance of losing my family over the decision that I had made.

I had been going to church since March 2014, and I loved being there. But after accepting Christianity and specifically, who God really is, church felt different. I always look forward to my favorite day of the week, Sunday, and my favorite part is singing to God how great He is and thanking Him for what He has done and is doing. I never thought that I would be able to sing to God, but now I look forward to singing along with everyone else in our church.

I am very grateful to my husband, Wes, because if he had not cared about me so much and had not wanted me to be in heaven with him, I would not have experienced the true God, my heavenly Father, His Son, Jesus Christ, and the Holy Spirit.

Appendix

Glossary of Quranic and Islamic Terms[1]

Abu—Father of (followed by eldest son or daughter).

Ali Ibn Abi Talib—Muhammad's cousin and son-in-law, who, according to the Sunni, became the fourth rightly guided caliph following Muhammad's death, but is considered by the Shia to be the first Imam.

Allah—In Arabic, a generic word for God. The context determines which God is being discussed.

Ayatollah—In Shia Islam, a title meaning "Sign of God," given to leading Islamic scholars and spiritual leaders in Iran.

Ayats—A word meaning "verses" (literally, "miracles") in the Qur'an. There are more than 6,000 in the Qur'an.

Baraka—Blessing from Allah.

Basmala—Every Surah in the Qur'an, except the ninth, begins with this Arabic term translated, "In the name of God, Most Gracious, Most Merciful."

Caliph/Caliphate—Dynastic rulers or leaders of the Muslim world—specifically in Sunni Islam, the *Rashidun* (four Rightly Guided), who took leadership following the death of Muhammad.

Dawah—To "invite" or "call" others to faith and submission to Allah, or Muslims to a purer form of Islam.

Fatwa—In Sharia law, an authoritative but nonbinding legal opinion given by a *mufti* (legal scholar).

Hadith—Authoritative reports of the sayings or actions of Muhammad as compiled by the companions of the prophet.

Hajar al-Aswad—Black stone (perhaps a meteorite) set in a silver ring on the outer east corner of the Kaaba in the Grand Mosque in Mecca, Saudi Arabia.

Hajj—One of the five pillars of Islam, a pilgrimage to Mecca lasting 7-12 days and ending with the Eid-ul-Adha (Feast of Sacrifice).

Hamas—Palestinian Islamic fundamentalist movement engaged in grassroots organizing and armed resistance and terrorism against Israel and its allies.

Hijab—Traditional Muslim women's veil to cover part of the face or body for the purpose of modesty or morality.

Houris—Beautiful dark-eyed companions in heaven (Surah 44:51-56; 52:20; 55:52-63; 74-76).

Ibn—"Son of."

Ilhad—Heresy often involving open rebellion or blasphemy against Allah.

Imam—In Sunni Islam, one who stands in front, a local spiritual leader or the one who conducts the *Jumu'ah* (Friday) prayer. In Shia Islam, regarded as one of the divinely inspired successors to Muhammad.

'Îsa—Jesus in the Qur'an, who is considered to be a prophet of

Allah but not the Son of God, not crucified, not resurrected, and not divine.

Jabr—Meaning "destiny," as in all things are ultimately under the authority of Allah and his will.

Jihad—Struggle, strive, or fight. Sometimes divided between the greater (personal struggle to submit to Allah) and the lesser (waging war to defend Islam).

Jinn—Creatures or "genies" made of fire, not clay (like humans), who have free will but are often less virtuous than humans and can influence them for good or evil.

Kaaba—The black cube-shaped "House of God" in Mecca, reported to date back to the time of Abraham of the Bible. In Muhammad's day, it reportedly housed 360 idols before Muhammad conquered Mecca in AD 630 to destroy the idols and repurpose it for Islamic worship during hajj.

Madrasa—A school where Islamic sciences or Quranic scriptures and ideologies are studied.

Mihrab—Niche in the wall of a mosque indicating Qibla (direction towards Mecca).

Minbar—A short flight of steps in a mosque used by Imams to stand on during sermons.

Mir'aj—Muhammad's "night journey" from Mecca to Jerusalem and back on Buraq, a winged horse or pegasus.

Masjid—A Muslim place of worship, a mosque.

Muezzin—The man who calls Muslims to the daily prayers (salat) from the minaret of a mosque.

Mufti—Muslim legal expert specializing in Sharia who gives rulings on spiritual, criminal, and civil issues.

Mujahid—One who practices jihad or "struggles" in worship of Allah or to support Islam.

Qadi—A judge in a Sharia court.

Qibla—The direction of Mecca, or more specifically the Kaaba, which Muslims bow toward during their daily prayers (salat).

Ramadan—The ninth lunar month in Islam, during which Muslims fast (sawm), abstaining from food and drink during daylight hours (sunrise to sunset).

Rashidun—See *Caliph/Caliphate.*

Salat—The five daily times of prayer, which Muslims recite in Arabic.

Sawm—The Muslim fast, abstaining from food or drink from sunrise to sunset, during Ramadan, the ninth lunar month.

Shah—A title given to rulers and kings in Persia (modern-day Iran).

Shahadah—The "confession" is the first pillar of Islam: "There is no God but Allah; and Muhammad is his Prophet." It is to be recited publically in Arabic to become Muslim.

Sharia—Quranic law and jurisprudence affecting every aspect of life—civil, criminal, and spiritual.

Shiite—Those who rejected the first three caliphs following the death of Muhammad. Opposing the Sunni, the Shia, "Party of Ali," recognized Muhammad's oldest male relative, Ali Ibn Abi Talib, as the only rightful leader of the Muslim people.

Sunnah—The teachings of Muhammad as shown by his practices or specific instructions and guidelines on an issue or practice. Sunnah is generally derived by study and analysis of the Hadith and Qur'an.

Sunni—Meaning "the Path" or "Way," Sunnis comprise the majority of Muslims, who accepted the rightly guided caliphs following the death of Muhammad and were opposed by the Shiite, party of Ali.

Surah—A chapter in the Qur'an. There are 114 surahs and more than 6,000 verses, called *Ayah*.

Sharia—Qur'anic law is the legal system of Islam and is the standard for both secular and religious law.

Ulema—Group of Muslim scholars recognized as having specialist knowledge of Sharia law and Islamic theology.

Umma—The Muslim community or people as a whole.

Zakat—"Alms" or tax, typically 2.5 percent of one's net worth, which is to be collected and given to those in need, such as widows, orphans, the homeless, and the oppressed.

Endnotes

CHAPTER 1: WHAT IS ISLAM?

1. 2010 US census: Between 2000 and 2010, Islam grew by 160 percent, from 1 million to 2.6 million, according to the decennial census released by the Association of Statisticians of American Religious Bodies in Chicago. Source: Mark Kellner, "Muslim Mormon growth spurts found," *Washington Times*, May 2, 2012, http://p.washingtontimes.com/news/2012/may/2/muslim-mormon-growth-spurts-found/?page=1 (accessed September 19, 2017).

2. Unless otherwise noted, all citations from the Qur'an are either from the translation by Muhammad Taqi al-Din al-Hilali and Muhammad Muhsin Kahn, *The Noble Qur'an in the English Language* (Riyadh: Darussalam Publishers, 1996), or the English translation by Abdullah Yusuf Ali, *The Holy Qur'an: Translation and Commentary* (Lahore, Pakistan: Shaikh Muḥammad Ashraf, 1934 and 1937).

3. "Say: He is Allah, the One and Only; Allah, the Eternal, Absolute; He begetteth not, nor is He begotten; And there is none like unto Him" (Qur'an, Surah 112:1-4). For more on this concept, see chapter 10.

4. For a more thorough definition of these key words, see John L. Esposito, *The Oxford Dictionary of Islam* (New York: Oxford University Press, 2003).

5. Muhammad was monogamous during his first marriage, but after Khadijah died, he took about a dozen wives and concubines. Khadijah was 15 years older than Muhammad, and his youngest wife, Aisha, was six years old when she married the Prophet. Their marriage was consummated when she was nine or ten. George W. Braswell, *Islam: Its Prophet, Peoples, Politics, and Power* (Nashville, TN: Broadman & Holman, 1996), 17.

6. Braswell, *Islam*, 17.

7. The largest branch of Shia Islam is the Twelver or Imami Shia Muslims. The name *Twelvers* comes from their belief that after Muhammad's death, Allah commissioned 12 successive Imams to lead the people. The final Imam vanished from history and is considered to be in hiding until his eventual return in the last days as the Mahdi (divinely guided deliverer). Approximately 85 percent of Shi'a are Twelvers. See Abdulwaheed Amin, "The Origins of the Sunni/Shi'a split in Islam," *Us Islam*, http://www.usislam.org/SunniShia/origins_of_the_sunni-shia%20split.htm (accessed February 11, 2018).

8. Fazlur Rahman, *Islam* (New York: Holt, Rinehart and Winston, 1968), xv-xxiii.

9. "Contemporary figures for Islam are usually between 1 billion and 1.8 billion, [but] 1 billion... appears to be dated, however." "Major Religions of the World Ranked by Number of Adherents," http://www.adherents.com/Religions_By_Adherents.html#Islam (accessed May 24, 2018).

10. Eric Pement, "The Ahmadiyya Movement in Islam" (2010), *Profile Notebook* (Arlington, TX: Watchman Fellowship, Inc., 1994–2018), www.watchman.org/profiles/pdf/ahmadiyyaprofile.pdf (accessed August 4, 2017).

11. Ron Carter, "The Nation of Islam" (1998), *Profile Notebook* (Arlington, TX: Watchman Fellowship, Inc., 1994–2018), www.watchman.org/profiles/pdf/nationofislamprofile.pdf (accessed November 12, 2017).

12. For a comprehensive history of Islam, see John L. Esposito, *The Oxford History of Islam* (New York: Oxford University Press, 1999).

13. The Qur'an mentions no specific number but states that every people group throughout world history has been given a prophet to warn them (35:24). See also "Twenty Five Prophets Mentioned in the Holy Qur'an," Irqa Islamic Publications, http://www.iqra.net/articles/muslims/prophets .php (accessed May 24, 2018).

14. The Qur'an affirms the Old Testament Torah as given to Moses (Surah 6:91), the Psalms of David (Surah 21:105), and the New Testament "gospel" (Surah 5:46-49).

15. Surah 3:44-47; 19:20.

16. *Oxford Dictionary of Islam*, 293, 317.

17. The Qur'an is vague about what actually happened at the crucifixion, saying only that people thought they had crucified 'Īsa, but "for of a surety they killed him not" (Qur'an 4:157-158). Later Muslim scholars speculated that someone else was substituted on the cross in place of Jesus—either Simon of Cyrene (Mark 15:21), Judas Iscariot, or one of the other disciples. See chapter 12 for more information.

18. Geisler and Saleeb, *Answering Islam*, 110-131.

19. Muslims believe that everyone is born Muslim until they are later led astray by wrong beliefs or other religions. Thus, Muslims often view conversion to Islam as a return or reversion to one's original faith. See also "How to Convert to Islam and Become a Muslim," http://www.islamreligion .com/articles/204/ (accessed May 24, 2018).

20. Muslims generally allow for some exceptions to fasting requirements for women who are pregnant, infants, travelers, etc. "Whoever breaks his fast without an excuse such as illness, travel he can never compensate this broken fast no matter how many days he fasts during his lifetime." Tirmizi, Nasai, Abu Davud, İbn Maja, İbn Huzayma, Ask a Question to Us, https://askaquestionto.us/ question-answer/ramadan/who-is-exempt-from-fasting (accessed May 24, 2018).

21. "From the Arabic root meaning 'to strive,' 'to exert,' 'to fight'; exact meaning depends on the context. May express a struggle against one's evil inclinations, an exertion to convert unbelievers, or a struggle for the moral betterment of the Islamic community." *Oxford Dictionary of Islam*, 159-60.

22. Surah 2:216; 8:38-39; 8:65-67; 9:123; and 47:4.

23. This concept is discussed more thoroughly in chapter 14. Chapter 15 contains a transcript of my two-hour debate on this subject, "Jesus Christ: Prophet of Allah or Savior of the World?" The debate was with Khalil Meek, executive director of the Muslim Legal Fund of America.

24. Even liberal New Testament scholars such as Bishop John Robinson concede that the Gospel records were written sometime between AD 40 and 60—well within the lifetime of the apostles. Many Muslims, however, reject the four New Testament Gospels in favor of the Gospel of Barnabas, which is actually a sixteenth-century forgery, as some Muslim scholars are now acknowledging. Geisler and Saleeb, *Answering Islam*, 217-220; 303-307.

25. This chapter is based in part on an earlier work: James Walker, "Islam" (2010), *Profile Notebook* (Arlington, TX: Watchman Fellowship, Inc., 1994–2018), https://www.watchman.org/profiles/ pdf/islamprofile.pdf.

CHAPTER 2: WHAT IS THE QUR'AN?

1. "Hira Cave," Ministry of Hajj Kingdom of Saudi Arabia, http://www.hajinformation.com/main/ m9504.htm (accessed February 7, 2018).

2. It is also during the ninth lunar month, Ramadan, that the sawm, or fast, takes place.

3. *Ayat*, in Arabic, means "verses"; but has associative meanings of "proofs, evidence, lessons, signs, miracles or revelations."

4. Don Richardson, *Secrets of the Koran* (Bloomington, MN: Bethany House, 2003), 92.

5. Richardson, *Secrets of the Koran*, 92.

6. Estimates range from 450 to 800 deaths of top reciters; the majority of scholars report 700. Shaih Bukhari does not list a specific number, only reporting that a number of reciters were killed (vol. 6, book 61, Hadith 509).

7. Arabic term meaning "guardian" or "memorizer." This is the name given to those who memorize the Qur'an.

8. Muhammad did not leave a plan of succession of leaders following his death. Therefore, when he died, there was a power struggle. Some thought the next-oldest male relative of Muhammad, Ali, should be the sole leader of the Muslim believers. Those who follow this thinking today are known as Shia, which means Party of Ali. Sunnis, however, countered that other trusted companions of Muhammed that were more mature should take the lead. These leaders became known as the rightly guided caliphs.

9. Norman L. Geisler and Abdul Saleeb, *Answering Islam* (Grand Rapids: Baker, 2002), 93-94.

10. Sahih Bukhari, vol. 6, book 61, no. 510.

11. A number of authentic Hadiths and sources cite open disputes over Uthman's recension. Some examples include Sahih al-Bukhari, vol. 4, 466; vol. 6, 478-479; As-Suyuti, Al-Itqan fii Ulum al-Qur'an, 138-139, 193; Ibn Abi Dawud, Kitab al-Masahif, 87; Muwatta Imam Malik, 64.

12. Surah 5:43; 6:114-115; 7:157; 18:27.

13. Farooq Ibrahim, "The Problem of Abrogation in the Quran," Answering-islam.org, http://www.answering-islam.org/Authors/Farooq_Ibrahim/abrogation.htm (accessed February 7, 2018).

14. The new covenant is spoken of throughout the Bible: Jeremiah 31:31-34; Mark 14:24; Luke 22:20; Romans 6:14; 7:6; 8:1-39; 11:27; 1 Corinthians 11:25; Hebrews 8:6-8,13; 9:11-15; 12:24.

CHAPTER 3: JESUS OF THE QUR'AN IS A PROPHET OF GOD

1. For a more complete list of the hundreds of Old Testament messianic prophecies fulfilled in the New Testament, see J. Hampton Keathley, III, "Messianic Prophecies" at Bible.org, https://bible.org/article/messianic-prophecies (accessed May 24, 2018).

CHAPTER 4: JESUS OF THE QUR'AN WAS BORN OF A VIRGIN

1. For example, Abdullah Yusuf Ali (1872–1953), who wrote one of the most widely used English translations of the Qur'an, explained that the mother of Jesus was a sister to Aaron only in a symbolic sense in that they were both born into priestly families. He wrote, "Aaron, the brother of Moses, was the first in the line of Israelite priesthood. Mary and her cousin Elisabeth (mother of Yahya) came from a priestly family, and were therefore, 'sisters of Aaron' or daughter of 'Imran (who was Aaron's father)." *The Holy Quran: Text, Translation and Commentary,* 3d ed. (Lahore, Pakistan: Shaik Muhammad Ashraf, 1938), note 2481, page 201.

CHAPTER 5: JESUS OF THE QUR'AN IS "THE WORD"

1. Imam Kamil Mufti, "The Descriptive Titles of Jesus in the Quran (Part 2 of 2): A 'Word' and 'Spirit' from God," The Religion of Islam, January 4, 2015, https://www.islamreligion.com/articles/229/descriptive-titles-of-jesus-in-quran-part-2/ (accessed May 24, 2018).

2. Mufti, "The Descriptive Titles."

3. Shabir Ally, "The Bible Denies the Divinity of Jesus," *A Brief Illustrated Guide to Understanding Islam*, https://www.islam-guide.com/ch3-10-1.htm (accessed May 28, 2018).

4. "That 'firstborn' must denote primacy over creation, and not just within creation, is indicated by the conjunction linking the two verses: He is 'firstborn of all creation *because* in him were created all things (τὰ πάντα),' that is, everything, the universe, the totality of created entities…" J.D.G. Dunn, *The Epistles to the Colossians and to Philemon: A Commentary on the Greek Text* (Grand Rapids, MI: William B. Eerdmans, 1996), 90.

CHAPTER 6: JESUS OF THE QUR'AN IS THE MESSIAH

1. Imam Kamil Mufti, "The Descriptive Titles of Jesus in the Quran (Part 1 of 2): 'The Messiah' and 'A Miracle,'" The Religion of Islam, January 4, 2015, https://www.islamreligion.com/articles/230/descriptive-titles-of-jesus-in-quran-part-1/ (accessed May 24, 2018).

2. Imam Kamil Mufti, "The Descriptive Titles of Jesus In the Quran (Part 1 of 2)."

3. N. Vasram and A. Toussi, *Mahdi in the Quran According to Shi'ite Quran Commentators* (Qum Islamic Republic of Iran: Ansariyan Publications, 2008).

CHAPTER 7: JESUS OF THE QUR'AN PERFORMED MIRACLES

1. For example, a very similar account of Jesus creating living birds out of mud figures is found in the "Infancy Gospel of Thomas" or "Gospel of the Infancy of Christ." This is an apocryphal story attributed to Thomas the Israelite, probably written in the middle to late second century CE and known to be in circulation in Arabia during the time of Muhammad. See G. Thomas, "Muhammad, the Qur'an, and Christian Sources," Answering Islam, http://www.answering-islam.org/Quran/Sources/cradle.html (accessed May 24, 2018).

2. Muslim apologists will sometimes appeal to several somewhat ambiguous passages in the Qur'an as evidence of Muhammad performing miracles. For example, it has been claimed that Muhammad split the moon in half and reassembled it based on Surah 54:1: "The Hour has drawn near, and the moon has been cleft asunder." Some Muslims even say the miracle has been scientifically validated either by a crack in the moon photographed by NASA or by similar "moon-splitting" and reassembling phenomena believed to have occurred on one of the moons of the planet Uranus. See Mohamed Ali, "Crack on moon confirms Prophet Muhammad (S) had split it," *Jafariya News,* http://www.jafariyanews.com/2k8_news/march/22moon_crack.htm. Also, Nabil Haroun, "Evidence of Moon Splitting," About Islam, http://aboutislam.net/counseling/ask-about-islam/evidence-moon-splitting/ (accessed May 24, 2018).

3. Bilal Philips, "Allah's challenge in the Quran to produce work similar," *IqraSense,* http://www.iqrasense.com/quran/allahs-challenge-in-the-quran-to-produce-work-similar-to-it.html (accessed May 24, 2018).

CHAPTER 8: JESUS OF THE QUR'AN WILL RETURN AGAIN IN THE END TIMES

1. Harun Yahya, IslamiCity.org, December 25, 2013, http://www.islamicity.org/5640/jesus-will-return/ (accessed February 7, 2018).

2. QuranX Hadith Collection, Sahih Bukhari, book 60, Hadith 118 (USC-MSA web [English]

reference, vol. 4, book 55, Hadith 657), http://quranx.com/Hadith/Bukhari/USC-MSA/Vol
ume-4/Book-55/Hadith-657/ (accessed May 24, 2018).

3. Sunan Abu-Dawud, "Battles (Kitab Al-Malahim)," book 37, http://quranmalayalam.com/hadees/
abudawud/037.sat.html (accessed May 24, 2018).

4. For more information on Shia eschatology, see the interview with Elijah, a former Shia Muslim
who became a Christian, in chapter 17 of this book. Also, see the four-page profile by Dr. Mike
Edens, "Shia Islam" (2012), *Profile Notebook* (Arlington, TX: Watchman Fellowship, Inc., 1994–
2018), http://www.watchman.org/profiles/pdf/shiaprofile.pdf (accessed November 30, 2017).

CHAPTER 9: JESUS OF THE QUR'AN IS "ANOTHER JESUS"

1. *Allah*, in Arabic, is simply a generic word for God. The context determines which God is being
discussed. In the Greek New Testament, the word for God is *Theos*. The same word *Theos* is used
to refer to the one true God (1 Timothy 4:5) and to "the God of this world" (2 Corinthians 4:4),
who is Satan. For a discussion of the use of Allah in Arabic Bible translations, see Michael Abd El-
Massih, "The Word Allah and Islam," Arabic Bible Outreach Ministry, https://www.arabicbible
.com/for-christians/1810-the-word-allah-and-islam.html (accessed May 24, 2018).

CHAPTER 10: JESUS OF THE QUR'AN IS NOT THE SON OF GOD

1. Joseph Cumming, "Is Jesus Christ the Son of God?—Responding to the Muslim view of Jesus,"
Enrichment Journal, Summer 2012, http://enrichmentjournal.ag.org/201203/201203_056_Jesus_
Son_of_God.cfm (accessed May 24, 2018).

2. Sarah Eekhoff Zylstra, "Wycliffe Associates Leaves Bible Translation Alliance over 'Son of God'
for Muslims," *Christianity Today,* March 7, 2016, http://www.christianitytoday.com/news/2016/
march/wycliffe-associates-leaves-wga-bible-translation-son-of-god.html (accessed May 24, 2018).

3. Gene Veith, "An inside perspective on the Islamic-friendly Bible," Pathos, March 22, 2012, http://
www.pathos.com/blogs/geneveith/2012/03/an-inside-perspective-on-the-islamic-friendly-bible/
(accessed May 24, 2018).

CHAPTER 11: JESUS OF THE QUR'AN IS NOT
THE SECOND PERSON OF THE TRINITY

1. Alan Cairns, *Dictionary of Theological Terms* (Greenville, SC: Ambassador Emerald International,
2002), 494.

2. "Tawhid" in *The Oxford Dictionary of Islam*, ed. John L. Esposito, Islamic Studies Online, http://
www.oxfordislamicstudies.com/article/opr/t125/e2356 (accessed January 24, 2018).

3. Paul P. Enns, *The Moody Handbook of Theology* (Chicago, IL: Moody, 1989), 641.

4. There are many other passages in the Qur'an that speak to the oneness and uniqueness of Allah.
For example, see 6:101; 19:89-93; 23; 39:62-63; 40:62; 42:11; 91; 112:1-4.

5. Modalism is "the view of the Trinity that denies personal distinctions in the Godhead and makes
Father, Son, and Holy Spirit to be three modes of operation of the same divine person, as creation,
redemption, and sanctification." Cairns, *Dictionary of Theological Terms*, 283.

6. Ibn Taymlya, "Trinity and Logic," Jesus-is-Muslim.net, October 5, 2013, https://jesus-is-muslim
.net/trinity-logic/ (accessed January 24, 2018).

7. Matthew 2:2,11; 8:2; 9:18; 14:33; 15:25; 20:20; 28:9; Mark 5:6; Luke 2:15; John 9:38; 12:20-21; 20:28; Hebrews 1:6.

8. Deuteronomy 6:4; Isaiah 43:10; 1 Timothy 2:5.

9. Father—Galatians 1:1; Son—John 1:1; Holy Spirit—Acts 5:3-4.

10. Matthew 3:16-17; Luke 22:42; John 14:16-17.

11. Ravi Zacharias International Ministries, "What is God really like: Tawhid or Trinity? Dr. Shabir Ally and Dr. Nabeel Qureshi Debate," filmed April 8, 2015, video at https://www.youtube.com/watch?v=FWpqqqZn7Kg&t=6438s (accessed May 24, 2018).

12. Al Mojadala, "Full Debate: Is Jesus God? Dr. Anis Shorrosh vs Sheikh Ahmed Deedat," filmed December 1985, video at https://www.youtube.com/watch?v=kXIBBCcJfRc (accessed May 24, 2018).

13. John Calvin as quoted in Cairns, *Dictionary of Theological Terms*, 495.

CHAPTER 12: JESUS OF THE QUR'AN WAS NOT CRUCIFIED ON THE CROSS

1. Eric Pement, "The Ahmadiyyab Movement in Islam," *Profile Notebook* (Arlington, TX: Watchman Fellowship, Inc., 1994–2018), www.watchman.org/profiles/pdf/ahmadiyyaprofile.pdf (accessed January 31, 2018).

2. John 19:34.

3. Abdullah Kareem, "The Crucifixion of Judas," Answering-Christianity.com, http://www.answering-christianity.com/abdullah_smith/crucifixion_of_judas.htm (accessed January 31, 2018).

4. Gary R. Habermas, *The Historical Jesus* (Joplin, MO: College Press, 1996).

5. Julius Africanus, *Chronography*, 18:1.

6. Tacitus 15.44.

7. This was written in a letter by Mara bar Serapion to his son.

8. Origen, *Against Celsus*, book 2, chapter 33.

9. Pliny, *Letters*, transl. William Melmoth, rev. W.M.L. Hutchinson (Cambridge: Harvard University Press, 1935), vol. II, X:96.

10. *Antiquities* 18.3.63-64.

11. Josephus, in addition to the reference above, made other reference to Jesus in *Antiquities* 20.9. The important issue here is the charge of Christian interpolation, primarily attributed to the fourth-century apologist Eusebius. Nevertheless, even taking out the "Christian" wording in the extant copies, one finds clear evidence that Jesus was believed to be the Messiah, was crucified, and his followers claimed that he had risen. There are three camps that scholars fall into regarding this issue. One very small group contends that the passage is original and entirely authentic; while another small group believes that it is entirely a Christian forgery. However, most scholars believe that the passage contains Christian interpolations in what was Josephus's original and authentic writing about Jesus. The majority of scholars accept this third position in large part due to a tenth-century copy of Josephus's works written in Arabic, which textual comparison supports his claims concerning Jesus minus the "Christian" wording.

12. Habermas, *The Historical Jesus*, 155.

CHAPTER 13: JESUS OF THE QUR'AN
DID NOT RISE FROM THE DEAD

1. Ibn Kathīr, 1:350, on Q 3.55-58, cited by G. Reynolds, "The Muslim Jesus: Dead or alive?" *Bulletin of the School of Oriental and African Studies* (2009), 72(2), 237-258, https://www.cambridge.org/core/journals/bulletin-of-the-school-of-oriental-and-african-studies/article/muslim-jesus-dead-or-alive/527849E7101E74FC672FB8B4F8AC5B07 (accessed May 24, 2018).

2. Habermas, *The Historical Jesus*, 158.

3. Al-Nasa'i, Al-Kubra, 6:489. This is considered an accurate and authentic Hadith.

4. Mahmoud M. Ayoub, "Towards an Islamic Christology II: The death of Jesus, reality or delusion (A study of the death of Jesus in Tafsir literature)," *The Muslim World*, Hartford Seminary (April 1980), 70 (2): 106.

5. Old Testament prophesies concerning the death of Jesus: Psalm 22:16; Isaiah 53:5-12; Zechariah 12:10. Old Testament prophecies concerning the resurrection of Jesus: Psalm 16:10; 49:15. Jesus prophesying of His death: Matthew 26:2; John 3:14; 6:70-71; 13:18-33. Jesus's own resurrection: Matthew 12:28-40; 16:4,21; 17:9,23; 20:17-19; Mark 8:31; 9:9,31; 10:32-34; Luke 9:22; 11:29-30; 18:31-34; John 2:19-22.

CHAPTER 14: JESUS OF THE QUR'AN IS
NOT THE SAVIOR OF THE WORLD

1. "Our One and Only Savior," Submission.org (2013), http://submission.org/One_and_Only_Savior.html (accessed January 22, 2018).

2. Among other differences, Islam teaches that Ishmael was the son being offered, whereas the Bible names Isaac as the son who was to be sacrificed. Christians have historically pointed out the foreshadowing of Abraham's symbolic sacrifice of his "only son" with God sacrificing His "only begotten Son" as an offering for sin. Abraham's prophecy to Isaac, "God will provide for Himself the lamb," was immediately fulfilled by the sacrificial ram (Genesis 22:13), but ultimately fulfilled when the "Lamb of God" was sacrificed for the sins of His people (John 1:29).

3. In the biblical account, God referred to Isaac as Abraham's "only son whom you love," although technically Abraham had both sons—Ishmael and Isaac. This further foreshadows later references to Jesus being called "His only begotten Son" (John 3:16) and receiving God's affirmation, "You are My beloved Son" (Mark 1:11).

4. Dick Staub, "Why Don Richardson Says There's No 'Peace Child' for Islam," *Christianity Today*, February 1, 2003, http://www.christianitytoday.com/ct/2003/februaryweb-only/2-10-22.0.html (accessed February 9, 2018).

5. "Salvation in Islam," Just Ask Islam, http://www.justaskislam.com/23/salvation-in-islam/ (accessed May 10, 2017).

6. For a discussion of some of the relevant Hadith narrations and an Islamic apologetic response, see Sam Shamoun, "Was Muhammad certain of his salvation?" Answering Islam, http://www.answeringislam.org/authors/shamoun/muhammad_salvation.html (accessed February 11, 2018).

CHAPTER 17: INTERVIEW WITH ELIJAH, FORMER SHIA MUSLIM

1. Elijah asked that his full name not be revealed for security reasons.

2. The Nestorians spread the theology of Nestorius, Archbishop of Constantinople (AD 386–451), who taught that the Christ consisted of two separate persons—one divine person and one human person—sharing the same body. This teaching violates the biblical teaching that Christ was one indivisible person who was both fully divine and fully human. Jesus was eternally God and never stopped being divine when He "became flesh and dwelt among us" (John 1:14). Nestorianism was officially condemned as heretical at the Council of Ephesus (AD 431).

3. Sahih al-Bukhari, Book of Revelation, Hadith (chapter 3) https://sunnah.com/bukhari/1/3. See also, *The History of al-Tabari: Muhammad at Mecca*, translated and annotated by W. Montgomery Watt and M.V. McDonald (Albany, NY: State University of New York Press, 1988), Volume VI, pp. 70-127, https://www.kalamullah.com/Books/The%20History%20Of%20Tabari/Tabari_Volume_06.pdf (accessed May 29, 2018).

APPENDIX: GLOSSARY OF QURANIC AND ISLAMIC TERMS

1. For a more thorough definition of these and other key words, see John L. Esposito, *The Oxford Dictionary of Islam* (New York: Oxford University Press, 2003).

To learn more about Harvest House books and
to read sample chapters, visit our website:

www.harvesthousepublishers.com

HARVEST HOUSE PUBLISHERS
EUGENE, OREGON